All Together Now

The co-living and co-working revolution

Naomi Cleaver
Amy Frearson

RIBA Publishing

© RIBA Publishing, 2021

Published by RIBA Publishing, 66 Portland Place, London, W1B 1AD

ISBN 978 1 85946 898 2

British Library Cataloguing-in-Publication Data
A catalogue record for this book is available from the British Library.

Commissioning Editor: Elizabeth Webster

Assistant Editor: Clare Holloway

Production: Richard Blackburn

Designed and typeset by Zoe Mercer

Printed and bound by Short Run Press, Exeter

Cover image © Naomi Cleaver

www.ribapublishing.com

Contents

About the sponsors

As proud joint sponsors of this publication, Project Interiors and Project FF&E offer a comprehensive fit out and furniture service that delivers distinctive 'shared space' projects; student accommodation, multi-family, build to rent, co-living, co-working, multi-gen.

Our deep technical expertise and wide-reaching partnerships combine with a relish for outstanding customer service to efficiently convert design vision into joyful, beautiful, enduring reality.

To find out more go to:
www.projectffe.com   www.projectinteriors.co.uk

Foreword

The concept of sharing has been a driving force in my life since childhood, its importance in architecture and design the backbone of my professional life. My father, Jack Morgan, was an architect. He spent a lot of his time unravelling the intricacies of building design in his desire to understand and improve people's lives. Not simply through wood and brick or stone, but through shared space, community and belonging.

I was brought up in a home that challenged the norm. My family lived in a commune set up by my grandfather. Beginning in the late 1940s, three families pooled their savings to buy a large house – many of which were sold cheaply after the war – and started an experiment in intergenerational co-living that I am still part of to this day. Both the social and physical architecture of my childhood taught me many things, from the value of sharing to the importance of looking after others. It was out of this learning that I set up the Quality of Life Foundation.

These lessons have recently resurfaced as the coronavirus pandemic provided apt, if trying, context for the subject of how to live and work in shared spaces. Being confined to relative isolation, our homes have become a measuring tool for what in life we value the most. The authors have been able to tackle this immense subject rigorously and creatively. Their survey holds a necessary blend of objectivity and relatability. A pitch perfect combination of human aspiration and pragmatism.

Through their exhaustive research, Naomi and Amy have been able to interrogate some of the most pertinent aspects of communal design. Different degrees and different models of sharing; the question of independence and its complex relationship with solidarity; the longevity and power of intergenerational living. They also consider the disparities between generations who could or couldn't afford to live in their own spaces, and the long-term impacts of this. This book insightfully tackles these subjects with empathy and rigor.

Having grown up with an architect, and having run an architecture practice, through boom and bust, build and breakdown, it has become clear to me that our greatest asset as both individuals and societies is our resilience. The strength we build over time is what puts us in greater stead to battle whatever lies ahead. And strength is proven to be more powerful in numbers. To share is to build strength. This is the greatest message this book can offer.

PROFESSOR SADIE MORGAN OBE
DIRECTOR OF dRMM,
CHAIR OF THE QUALITY OF LIFE FOUNDATION

Fig 0.0.1 Communal dining area in Cohost West Bund Shanghai, by AIM Architecture, 2018

Introduction

The shift towards sharing

The definitions of 'home' and 'workplace' are blurring. With rising property prices impacting the affordability and livability of cities around the world, lifestyles becoming increasingly mobile, and loneliness considered a major health problem, we are finding new ways to live and work more closely together.

People of all ages and backgrounds – not just young people, but couples, families and pensioners too – are exploring the benefits of shared living. This is fuelling the emergence of radical new building typologies, designed around a concept of communal spaces and resources. These designs show that sharing doesn't have to mean compromise, but can instead lead to more liberating and fulfilling lifestyles. Why waste money on a washing machine you only use once a week? Why cook every night when you can take turns with others? Why tie yourself to one location when you can work remotely anywhere?

Co-living and co-working are two of the words we use to describe these new shared living environments, but there are others too, like multigenerational, co-housing or build-to-rent. The degree of sharing differs for each, but they all have one thing in common: they are designed around the concepts of fluidity and flexibility, using economies of scale to offer higher-quality facilities and services than would otherwise be available. In some cases these resources simply offer greater convenience, but in others they facilitate more aspirational lifestyles. They can include anything from a communal kitchen or garden to a fully equipped gym or a diverse events programme. In many cases the fluidity extends to the contractual elements as well as the design; you might be able to move between locations or alter your setup if your situation changes.

Even now, as we come to terms with the impact of the COVID-19 pandemic, the trend for shared living spaces is showing no signs of slowing down. Instead of driving people apart, social distancing and a reliance on digital communication have led to a huge demand for physical togetherness. In a world where virtual exchanges – emails, video calls and social media – have become the go-to methods of communication, buildings and spaces that facilitate meaningful face-to-face interactions have become more valuable to us than ever. At the same time, those of us occupying small single-person homes without any outside space are reassessing whether living alone is all it's cracked up to be.

Co-living is not a new idea, of course. Humans are naturally gregarious creatures who have always recognised that there is safety (and sociability) in numbers. Examples of communal living can be found throughout history, for example in Ancient Greece, medieval times and the Stone Age. The single-family home is actually the more recent concept, bound up with the 20th-century ideology of the nuclear family.[1] In 19th-century North America, boarding houses provided a springboard for young men and women ready to leave the family home but yet to marry.

The century-old kibbutzim settlements, many of which still exist in Israel today, formed communities around agriculture and industry. Meanwhile in Denmark, the co-housing communes of the 1960s and 1970s offered alternatives to traditional family structures. The same goes for co-working, which finds precedents in the artist workshops of 15th-century Italy, or the 'golden age of libraries' in the 17th and 18th centuries.

What's different about the new shared living movement is that it is a global phenomenon built on new financial models as well as architectural typologies. From the ground up, groups of individuals are finding ways to collectively create buildings and spaces that suit their lifestyles and situations better than what the market offers. At the same time, new businesses are being set up specifically to build and manage communities. These companies provide the infrastructure to bring people together – the living or work environment – then package it up with desirable extras to create a readymade lifestyle product. Drawing on the service industry, they are creating homes that function like hotels, and workplaces that behave like coffee shops or social clubs.

The rise of co-living is being driven by a multitude of factors, with one of the most pressing being population growth. The number of us living in cities is rising all the time – an extra 2.5 billion are expected to move to urban areas by 2050.[2] As the demand for affordable housing increases, so too do property prices, making housing unaffordable for low-income workers and young people. Shared living offers a way to make buildings more space-efficient, and in return more cost-effective.

However, the trend is as much explained by distinctive social shifts as it is by the unaffordability of home ownership. More than ever, we are on the move to find new places to live, work and study. We are less likely to find a husband, wife or long-term partner until later in life (if at all), and divorce is increasingly common. This means that single-person households are becoming more prevalent worldwide and reports of a 'loneliness epidemic' frequently hit the headlines. It's not difficult to see how sharing models offer a solution. Being single and independent doesn't necessarily mean we want to give up the sense of solidarity offered by a parental or marital home, nor the standard of living that goes with it.

The influence of technology plays a crucial role here too. With mobile devices becoming rapidly more advanced, the number of people working remotely has been steadily growing for the past two decades; for instance, the US saw an increase of 159% between 2005 and 2017.[3] These numbers reached unprecedented levels during the COVID-19 pandemic of 2020, when millions were asked to work from home for the first time. Businesses were given proof of what the research has long suggested: that workers are more productive and take fewer sick days when they are away from the office.[4] Going forward, remote working looks set to become a continual trend for employed workers as well as freelancers. For many people, this means a fixed address is no longer needed – it's possible to co-live or co-work in any location, providing you have a laptop and a wifi connection. You could have a lifestyle where you're constantly moving from place to place, but it could be more nuanced, such as balancing time between a city life and a family home.

Technology has also facilitated the rise of the so-called 'sharing economy', allowing the concept of subscription-based sharing to infiltrate our everyday lives. Brands like Uber, Airbnb and Zipcar have created a model for how the sharing of both goods and services can be managed via smartphone apps, and made it enticing to a global audience. The jump from this to the sharing of space or property seems a clear and natural progression.

Although co-living is not specific to young people, they are the ones driving the trend. With the prospect of home ownership particularly bleak for those in their twenties and thirties, those in this age bracket are becoming increasingly mobile and less focused on the ownership of material possessions. Freed from the burden of furniture or household appliances, they are taking advantage of the opportunities to move around and travel. Some have experience of sophisticated student housing, so are demanding the same level of quality and fluidity from their homes when they move into full-time work.

At the other end of the generational spectrum, wealthy and healthy retirees are proving that co-living isn't just a young person's game. By downsizing from the family home, they are benefiting from the liberty, amenities and sociability offered by purpose-built accommodation, while releasing much-needed housing back into the market.

Pushing these polarities aside is intergenerational living, which has emerged in multiple ways: those in their twenties and thirties returning to the parental home to save for their own property, those in their thirties to fifties seeking familial support after a relationship breakdown, or multiple generations opting to live together so that younger members can care for those in advanced age (and sometimes vice versa). In the UK alone, a staggering 3.4 million people between the ages of 20 and 34 live in the parental home, a figure that has risen more than 25% since the turn of the 21st century.[5] But the trend also extends beyond the family, as retirement homes start to offer accommodation to students, and new designs for multifamily communities gain traction. Together, these alternative models are raising expectations of what co-living can be.

Co-working has even greater mass appeal. As workplace designer Sevil Peach points out, 'the more we become free to work wherever we want, the more we need an office'.[6] However, the form that office takes is ever-changing. Over the past decade we have seen brands like WeWork and Impact Hub completely disrupt the cultural norms of where and how we work, facilitating the rapid growth of freelance and entrepreneurial culture. For a monthly membership fee, these spaces offer all the perks of the office – from networking opportunities to printing facilities – without the inflexibility of being tied to a desk from nine to five, Monday to Friday. A new breed of co-working spaces is pushing this idea even further. Some offer access to multiple locations, so you can work just as easily when travelling. Some offer impressive events programmes, while others help their members to juggle busy lifestyles, with services ranging from childcare to wellness classes.

With the COVID-19 situation still fresh in our minds, the flexibility and sociability of the workspace becomes even more meaningful. We want going to the office to be a choice rather than an obligation, regardless of whether we work for ourselves or a company. As a result, the pressure is on for employers to maintain the benefits enjoyed by those who have worked remotely during the pandemic. Major organisations like the BBC and Sky have already proven that co-working design models can foster innovation in a company headquarters, while others have shown that opening up their spaces to freelancers and startups can facilitate a vibrant exchange of ideas. An increasing number of companies will be looking to house their staff in co-working spaces rather than permanent offices, and remote working will become a norm. Allied to this are financial benefits, as organisations no longer have to commit to long, expensive leases, and are able to expand, contract or shift location on demand.

Shared living is more than just a passing trend. It is rooted in our history and offers very real solutions to many of the problems we face today, both as individuals and as a society. It suggests how we might find ways to live more efficiently, healthily and sustainably in the future, without limiting our choices and comforts. But to get there, we need design models to show us the way. With that in mind, this book addresses the challenges and opportunities that co-living and co-working present to architects and interior designers. It outlines how spaces can be designed to be attractive and multifunctional, to promote wellbeing and flexibility, and to encourage collaboration and creativity. Case studies explore effective design solutions, while a design toolkit offers guidance for best practice. Co-living and co-working are here to stay; now is the time to define how we design for them.

Naomi Cleaver: designing for people

My practice as an interior designer is firmly couched in my fascination with the way buildings make us feel; a childhood lived in 13 different homes and seven different schools will do that. And, no doubt, the fluidity in my formative domestic environment is what drove me to initially specialise in designing homes.

The idea of 'home' is at the heart of the first student accommodation scheme I designed: iQ Shoreditch in east London in 2011. The community here was expected to be largely international, students away from their family home for the first time, and often thousands of miles distant. I strongly felt my task as interior designer was primarily pastoral, and so the scheme pivoted on a collection of shared kitchens and dining spaces where students from different backgrounds could come together over a comforting meal – always a positive platform – sharing their culture and getting to know new ones.

This project led me to develop my specialism in designing spaces where groups of people live and work together. Initially student accommodation, my studio now also works on co-live and co-work, including build-to-rent. The abiding lessons I've learned are, number one, never forget the individuals at the heart of a scheme built for many (nor forget their hearts), and number two, common sense is your most effective tool.

On large schemes especially, it can be easy to submit to the machine-led materialisation of a building and get lost in the intense and intensely regulated construction process. This is why I set up my own workshop, alongside my design studio practice, to support the vital role that adventure, imagination – daring even – and craft have to play in creating places that nourish the human soul, on budgets that cash-sensitive clients can sustain.

For me, design is a people business. It's being curious about how people 'work', and how to help them 'work' the best they can in the world we live in. As I write this, in autumn 2020, the world we live in is facing unique challenges, to put it mildly. Irrespective of whether you believe climate change is anthropogenic or not, what is incontrovertible is the evidence that human beings are exploiting natural resources on an increasingly populous planet, compromising habitats for our fellow species, the survival and health of which are symbiotic with our own.

The recent pandemic, and the concomitant evisceration of economies, has intensified questions about how we live and work together, and how we use resources. Loneliness, isolation, alienation and a disconnection from nature are all as much of a threat to our health as any virus.

The time for being more efficient with the way we share resources is now. The time for rethinking ways to live

and work together is now. The time to be bold, when our instinct might be to retreat, is now. Change is often painful. But as the external forces that activate change can rarely be simply resisted, the best defence we have is creativity.

We need to be the change.

This book was commissioned before the pandemic, but catalogues real-life solutions to these now acute problems. It not only spotlights new and seductive concepts of the social collective, but features projects that are already beginning to reinvent our built environment.

Designing social space in an age of social distancing is an intellectually stimulating but emotionally woeful challenge. Designers are working quickly to respond with contactless surfaces and hand-sanitising stations, screening and revised navigational routes, so we can be kept apart. I fervently hope this is temporary, and that the imposition of the state on our private lives is just the shock we need to think hard about the society we want, about the society we need if we are to thrive as individuals throughout our lives. The pandemic has accelerated the erosion of nuanced debate, proliferated the narcissism of identity politics and escalated the willing sacrifice of personal responsibility.

We urgently need to find ways to retexture society, for all of us to come together, with humility. The design of how and where we live and work is, I believe, a very good place to start.

Fig 1.0.0 The Italian Building, London, by Stiff + Trevillion and Studio Clement for Mason & Fifth, 2019

1.
Our new shared habitats

Co-living and co-working: a lexicon

The first thing to establish when designing a shared living or working environment is what exactly it is. Or, just as importantly, what it isn't. Co-living and co-working are both relatively new words, even though the concepts have been around for centuries, and they are often used to describe a myriad of different structures. But they aren't all-encompassing; their interpretations differ from some other new types of shared spaces, which come under other categories and titles. It can be challenging to navigate the subtle differences in terminology; in some cases, they relate to variations in architecture in design, but they can also refer to different types of financial or organisational systems. There are also some conflicting interpretations – for instance, co-living is often used as an umbrella term to refer to all the different types of shared living, but it also describes a very specific form of serviced rental accommodation. The list of terms here is by no means exhaustive, but it offers a starting point to help you understand what you're dealing with.

Co-living

Any form of residence where three or more biologically unrelated people live under the same roof can be defined as co-living. The term is also used more specifically to refer to rental accommodation that offers 'living as a service', meaning it operates more like a hotel than a residence. Here, tenants typically rent a furnished bedroom or micro-flat, but they also have access to shared living spaces and premium services.

Co-working

A more definitive term, co-working refers to any office or workspace that is either wholly or partially shared between three or more individuals or companies. Most co-working spaces are owned and managed by a landlord and operate on a rental or membership basis, but they can also be cooperatively owned.

Co-housing

Co-housing communities are created and managed by their residents. These developments include communal spaces, such as shared gardens or common houses, but residents also have their own self-contained private homes.

Cooperative

Homes or workplaces that are owned and managed collectively by occupants are known as cooperatives. Co-housing communities are typically cooperatives, but the terms are not interchangeable.

Build-to-rent

Build-to-rent (BTR) is a type of purpose-built residential designed specifically for private rental. Developments include at least 50 homes, owned and managed by a single landlord. They don't usually fall under the category of co-living, although tenants all have access to shared amenities and premium services, in addition to self-contained homes.

Serviced apartments

A model that has been around for decades, serviced apartments are rented homes where occupants have access to premium services. Unlike build-to-rent, serviced apartments don't necessarily come with shared amenities, which clearly sets them apart from co-living.

Purpose-built student accommodation

An upgrade to halls of residence, purpose-built student accommodation (PBSA) is a type of student housing built by private developers. It matches the co-living model, giving students a furnished bedroom or studio flat, plus use of communal spaces and services.

Multigenerational home

Any private residence that allows at least two adult generations to live at the same address can be called a multigenerational home. Typically these homes are occupied by families, where grandparents live with their children and grandchildren. They often have additional entrances and living spaces, as well as the necessary extra bedrooms.

Multifamily housing

Any residential development that allows several families to live in the same building or group of buildings, but in separate units, can be called multifamily housing. It can be used to refer to co-housing or build-to-rent models, but can also apply to more traditional apartment buildings and housing estates.

Intergenerational senior living

A term still being defined, intergenerational senior living refers to retirement facilities where elderly people live among people of other generations. It could be a care home offering free housing to students, or a facility set within an existing community, so that seniors regularly interact with children and families. The primary aim is to reduce social isolation.

Agrihood

An agrihood is a form of eco-village, where farming is integrated into the environment. Residents typically live in self-contained homes, but they produce the majority of their own food as a community. Some are also self-sufficient in terms of energy use.

Sharing comes in many forms

Sharing can manifest in the home or workplace in a number of ways, which is another reason why co-living and co-working can be difficult to categorise. The things you share might be physical, in the form of spaces or objects, but you might also share organisational structures or services, which will have a different impact on the look and feel of the physical environment. In some setups almost everything is communal, but the degree of sharing could be more minimal. For example, if you lived in a private apartment but shared a garden with your neighbours, you probably wouldn't call it co-living, although it's certainly a step in that direction. But what about if you added on other amenities, like a communal laundry room, or a common kitchen? At what point does the definition change? The boundaries are equally blurred when it comes to workspaces. If several startups rent private offices in a building with shared meeting rooms and a kitchen, is it co-working? Or does there need to be more on offer, like a communal lounge or events space?

There is no definitive answer to these questions, but the more you understand the range of options on offer, the more possibilities open up to you as an architect or designer. There are four categories that sharing systems can fall under:

Spaces

Shared physical space is of course fundamental to the design of co-living and co-working environments. Any shared living or working space must include some portion of space (large or small) which is communal without being open to the general public. This can include spaces that are bookable, such as meeting rooms or spare bedrooms.

Resources

All objects and consumables fall under the category of shared resources, so naturally most co-living and co-working spaces will include a number of them. Typical shared objects include kitchen appliances, tools and electronic devices, along with forms of transport like pool cars and bicycles. Food and drink can also be shared, in the form of communal meals or community agriculture. Sharing of resources has obvious implications for physical space requirements – the more you share, the less personal space you are likely to need.

Services

Shared services are most often included when the living or working setup is based on a hospitality model. Cleaning, laundry and maintenance services are common, but some places also offer their occupants access to

events, classes or subscription services like Netflix and Spotify. Co-living venues often offer access to co-working spaces. Not all services are included; some come in the form of paid-for extras, with convenience in mind.

Contracts

Ownership and management are highly important to the way a co-living or co-working model operates. Some setups work under democratic systems, while others have a centralised approach with opportunities for feedback built in. With the introduction of sophisticated digital networks and platforms, these management systems can become incredibly complex, linking people across wider networks of spaces.

Are we ready to share?

Thanks to digital sharing platforms like Airbnb and Zipcar, we've all become more comfortable with the concept of sharing over the past decade, yet there is still a stigma attached. Many still see sharing as a compromise, with co-living and co-working included by association. But almost everyone is open to sharing something, as proven by One Shared House 2030, an ongoing online survey by research studios Space10 and Anton & Irene. More than 154,000 people (and counting) have so far filled out the survey, from over 150 countries, and only 3% said they wouldn't share anything in their home.[1]

In fact, the things we are and aren't willing to share can vary significantly from person to person. According to One Shared House, 39% of us would willingly share a kitchen, 56% would share laundry facilities, 34% would share a car and a surprising 22% of us would share a toilet. This is because the choices we make in relation to the way we live our lives are as much fuelled by emotions as they are by rationality. For instance, some of us associate the car with a sense of personal freedom or achievement, while for others it is merely a means of getting from A to B. A set of tools might be something you value, particularly if they have been passed down through generations, but you could just as easily form an emotional attachment to a new vacuum cleaner.

More important than the types of things being shared is the clarity that accompanies them, or so the research suggests. People are generally open to a mix of private and shared spaces – 'we spaces' and 'me spaces' – providing that the terms of use are clearly defined and the systems within which the spaces operate function well.

Things are better when we come together

Co-living and co-working offer benefits both at a personal level, and to society and the environment at large. They fall under six categories:

Affordability

Shared space always offers cost savings in some form, thanks to economies of scale. For those on a low income, for whom home ownership has become an increasingly unattainable goal, sharing a home with others makes it possible to live in a city without spending the majority of your wages on rent. For those

with a little bit more to spend, it can mean access to luxuries that you would never otherwise be able to afford, like a swimming pool, a library or a cinema screening room. The same rules apply to co-working.

Health and happiness

It has been proven that loneliness and social isolation contribute to mental health issues, dementia and premature death.[2] With more of us living alone and, thanks in part to the COVID-19 pandemic, more of us now working from home, the odds are stacked against us when it comes to the likelihood of us living healthily and happily. With more varied opportunities for sociability, co-living and co-working offer an obvious solution. In addition, sites with health and fitness facilities included can certainly help us along the way.

Choice and flexibility

Economies of scale don't just lead to financial benefits; they also open up access to a greater choice of space and facilities. As the trend for co-living and co-working gains pace, the variety of offerings continues to expand and diversify. It's now possible to choose the size of community you're comfortable in, the type of people you want to be around and the activities available to you. In co-living for instance, there are setups built specifically around travel opportunities or wellness.

Safety and security

Since the dawn of time, the principal benefit of being part of a community has been the safety that comes

Fig 1.0.1 and 1.0.2 Communal living and working spaces at Cumberland Place, Southampton, designed by Naomi Cleaver

with it. When you regularly interact with others day-to-day, it means you naturally have someone around to call on if and when you need support. While that brings certain limitations about how you can behave – it means you have to be respectful of others – it can also bring greater freedoms. Being able to call on a neighbour or share responsibilities with them offers time- and cost-saving benefits.

Diversity

At a time when it's very easy to listen only to the views of people who agree with us, we increasingly need spaces that – unlike the Facebook echo chamber – offer us exposure to alternative experiences and perspectives. Shared live/work spaces have a powerful role to play in bringing together people of different ages, races and backgrounds, and helping to promote greater understanding, empathy and tolerance.

Sustainability

With concern for the environment growing, we are becoming increasingly aware of our carbon footprint. Living and working together more densely is one of the biggest ways in which we can contribute to the sustainability of our buildings and cities. The construction industry is the largest contributor to energy use, accounting for 39% of all carbon emissions worldwide.[3] By creating homes and workplaces that use space more efficiently, this figure could be reduced.

Obstacles to overcome

Despite the benefits, there are some major barriers when it comes to planning shared buildings, which have particular resonance for co-living rather than co-working. While we consider co-living and co-working to be part of the same family, it's important to remember that co-working is streets ahead of co-living in terms of uptake and popularity. The co-working movement did begin a decade earlier – San Francisco-based engineer Brad Neuberg is widely credited to have started it in 2005, while the term co-living didn't enter general use until around 2014. But that's not the only reason it's more widespread.

Thanks to the modern open-plan office, shared workspace is a concept that will have been familiar to many long before co-working came around. But with single-person households continuously on the rise – there are more than eight million in the UK alone, and over 300 million worldwide – the idea of shared living is more of an unknown, particularly outside the constructs of the parental or marital home.[4] As a result, privacy has become our number one concern in the home, and a major barrier to co-living and its perception.

This trend was highlighted in the 2019 edition of the *IKEA Life at Home Report*, an annual report that explores trends in modern domestic life.[5] According to the stats, 85% of people believe they have a right to privacy in the home, yet 23% of people already feel their concerns around privacy are not met. Even those of us who share homes with partners or family struggle to find space of our own. So it's not surprising that people might associate co-living with a further strain on privacy.

What the report does identify however is that privacy can be found through many different activities and can take place in all kinds of different spaces. In a world where social media makes it harder for people to switch off, a feeling of privacy is not necessarily about being alone. It's simply about finding our own opportunities for recovery, relaxation and focus. For any new co-living development to be successful, it must demonstrate its ability to provide these three things. It must include private spaces that are clearly off-limits to others, and it must create barriers to prevent privacy intrusions.

Another barrier to co-living comes in the form of building regulations. In many countries, it can be difficult to gain planning permission for co-living buildings, because they don't fall under traditional use categories – they don't meet the standards set out for residential, which were drawn up with traditional houses and apartments in mind. There are workarounds: some developers have gained planning permission for co-living by converting office buildings, which can be possible under permitted development (PD) rights relating to 'change of use', while others have secured permission by mixing long and short stays, allowing them to meet the criteria for a hotel. In the future, though, co-living needs more government support at a planning level in order to progress.

Thriving after the pandemic

It may seem strange to be exploring the benefits of co-living and co-working in the aftermath of the COVID-19 pandemic. The concept of living and working more closely with others is completely at odds with the social distancing that has recently become a societal norm. But in fact, one of the big outcomes of our experience with the virus has been a renewed spirit of community and togetherness. As George Monbiot puts it: 'The horror films got it wrong. Instead of turning us into flesh-eating zombies, the pandemic has turned millions of people into good neighbours'.[6] Instead of hiding away, people around the world have been doing all they can to connect with and support those around them. There are stories everywhere of virtual playdates, grocery deliveries, meal sharing, volunteer drivers and neighbourhood music performances. Quite simply, being separated from friends, family and colleagues made us realise how much we value our relationships with others.

There were numerous reports from established co-living communities detailing the ways that occupants came together during periods of national lockdown.[7] There was no mass exodus; instead the evidence suggests that co-living residents were largely grateful to have a live-in community at a time when they were cut off from the outside world. While single-person households faced issues of prolonged isolation, and family homes were mostly ill-equipped to provide separation for vulnerable members, co-living was able to get around both issues. With many offering a balanced mix of private rooms (where residents could isolate themselves) and shared spaces (where social distancing measures could be enforced), occupants could maintain social bonds without putting themselves at risk.

Looking ahead, we can expect to see an increased interest in the home and the scope of what it can offer through economies of scale. Gardens, balconies and study areas may have been a luxury in the past but now they are essentials, and even better if you can have both private and shared versions. We can also anticipate the growth of 'conscious co-living', a newly defined form of shared living that prioritises 'connection and flourishing'. With a focus on three elements – wellbeing, community and sustainability – it proposes that co-living can allow individuals and collectives to not only share resources, but also an intention of living sustainably and harmoniously with each other and the planet.[8]

Co-working fared much worse during the pandemic, with the majority of spaces forced to close and occupants given no choice but to work from home. As social distancing measures were eased and spaces reopened, large corporate co-working operators like WeWork and Regus found it hard to entice occupants to return. Stories emerged about huge office spaces turning into ghost towns.[9] The concept of hot-desking was too hard a sell to those who could just as easily work from home. But the demand for co-working hasn't disappeared; rather it's shifted focus. We've learned which tasks can be more successfully carried out at home, and which ones need people to be physically together. As a result, the role of the office has changed from being primarily a place of work to becoming a hub of collaboration and connectivity. The co-working spaces that have been able to adapt to this are the ones where community was already a primary focus, and where flexible use is welcomed.

Looking ahead, the new remote working model looks set to continue among both freelancers and companies, which means that co-working is likely to bounce back even stronger than before. The more people switch to this lifestyle, the easier it will be for spaces to offer the flexibility demanded. But as with co-living, shared workspaces look set to change from completely communal models to those that include both 'we spaces' and 'me spaces'. We can also expect a shift towards the cluster model, where large groups are broken down into smaller collectives, to foster more of a community spirit.

Fig 2.0.0 Student dining room at IQ Shoreditch, with interior design by Naomi Cleaver, 2011

2.
Student housing reinvented

Things can only get better

The new model of purpose-built student accommodation (PBSA) laid the foundations for the co-living movement. Student housing is the form of co-living that is most likely to be familiar to people, but the 'halls of residence' of the past pale in comparison to some of the student accommodation on offer today.

Turn the clock back 20 years, and student living was a completely different story. Students would rent accommodation through universities, often ending up in bland and uninspiring dormitories, with little more than a pinboard to express their personality. The quality was generally poor, with lodgings typically consisting of a single or shared bedroom, access to kitchen and bathroom facilities, and not a lot else. An internet connection would have been a luxury. Today however, student housing is an incredibly competitive market where private developers, as well as the universities themselves, are battling to attract student interest. PBSA offers students exciting spaces and services that allow these term-time homes to become destinations in their own right.

According to Frank Uffen, co-founder of nonprofit think tank The Class of 2020, this change was primarily fuelled by the increase in global mobility. With more and more students looking to travel to new cities or even countries to study, universities found themselves competing for the same pool of applicants. 'The availability of English-taught university programmes in cities like Amsterdam or Barcelona started growing very fast, and that made it possible for a whole new generation of talent to move to new territories,' he explains. In the UK, things also changed greatly when the government removed the cap on the total number of students that universities could accept, meaning schools could target much bigger audiences.

With universities struggling to meet housing demand for these new arrivals, PBSA emerged as a practical solution. But in time, the quality of this accommodation became an important element of a university's proposition. By offering design-led living spaces, lesser-known cities like Warsaw or Munich could become new hotspots for international students. At the same time, big cities like London and Berlin could expand their markets.

Finding the right balance

Key to the success of PBSA is a balance between space efficiency and design quality. Just like student housing of the past, developments have to rely on compact spaces and sharing in order to make the numbers stack up. But at the same time, their offering has to be substantive enough to make it attractive. Students are no longer just tenants; they are consumers looking to find the right product. Design is essential to achieving this, as proven by companies like Greystar and Scape, who teamed up with leading architects and interior designers to pioneer the model at an international scale.

They did this in two ways.

First, bedrooms were reinvented as micro-homes, able to facilitate various different activities. 'It wasn't about making a tiny room and then filling it with furniture,' explains Ab Rogers, who developed the interior design for Scape's properties in the UK and Australia. The trick was to treat the entire space as a design object, allowing elements to take on dual functions. 'When you start to design in additional functions, you can create a more ambiguous language that is easy for people to customise to their own needs,' he says.

Second, communal spaces were reimagined as hubs of activity. No longer just functional, kitchens, lounges and study areas became meeting spaces, where you could work or hang out with friends. iQ Shoreditch, a Naomi Cleaver project from 2012, was one of the very first examples of this.

'If you design very small spaces, then you need to design bigger spaces that people can move into and decompress,' says Rogers. 'Common areas are key; you're trying to get people coming together, cooking together and socialising.'

The new frontier of student living

With the market for PBSA showing no signs of slowing down (even after the pandemic), developments are becoming increasingly sophisticated in terms of both design and business model. Our case studies Chapter King's Cross and BaseCamp Leipzig, as well as two Naomi Cleaver projects, The Project at Hoxton and

Fig 2.0.1 At Scape Swanston, in Melbourne, Ab Rogers turned student bedrooms into compact micro-homes, with plenty of natural light and no space wasted

Calico, show how far the typology has developed. Spaces are typically fully furnished, including everything from desk lamps to kitchen utensils, meaning students no longer have to worry about providing these things themselves. Large-scale complexes often host events programmes, allowing residents to meet one another, engage with local communities and network with potential employers. Wellness is also a key focus, with many venues offering gym facilities and classes.

Looking ahead, architects like BIG and WilkinsonEyre are showing how student housing can adapt to innovations in building technology, while companies like The Student Hotel – another of our case studies – are demonstrating

how it can move into other sectors, like hospitality. With so many exciting prospects, it was only natural that these concepts would start to incorporate other age groups besides young people. Students are not the only ones looking to benefit from more sociable and flexible lifestyles, so many PBSA developments now also include a portion of build-to-rent. According to Uffen, who is also a partner in The Student Hotel, the blending of students and other people was inevitable. 'We're always surprised by how many students are already entrepreneurs, doing a degree while running a couple of companies,' he says. 'Their lives are already blended; quite frankly, I think we're just catching up.'

Fig 2.0.2 At The Shield in Newcastle, Naomi Cleaver used custom joinery and furniture to create multifunctional amenity spaces for students

Fig 2.0.3 BIG's Urban Rigger offers a prototype for how shipping containers can be used to create shared living spaces on water rather than land. Twelve students each have their own private spaces, but a shared winter garden allows them to come together

Fig 2.04 Designed by creative agency Staat, The Student Hotel's Amsterdam West venue was one of the first examples of how student living could be combined with a hotel

Case study: Chapter King's Cross

Operator: Chapter Living

Client: Greystar

Architect/Interior designer: Tigg + Coll Architects

Type: Purpose-built student accommodation and build-to-rent

Location: London, UK

Completion year: 2016

Gross internal floor area: 2,000sqm

It used to be common in London for students to live in dorm-style accommodation for the first year of their studies, but to then find an alternative, such as a shared house with a group of friends. At Chapter King's Cross, occupants are not only motivated to stay in halls of residence for the duration of their studies, but to also consider how this form of co-living might suit them as they enter employment. With both welcoming common areas and top-of-the-range facilities, it promotes a lifestyle that might become hard to give up.

This building was previously used by another student housing operator before Chapter Living took it over. Tigg + Coll Architects was brought in to consider how it might better suit its purpose. The London-based studio focused on the common areas and how they might become more functional and aspirational. The aim was to create spaces that residents would genuinely want to use, but which would also bring in outsiders, not just fellow students but also community groups and business organisations. 'When you have all these people living here, you need something to really engage them,' explains studio co-founder David Tigg, 'otherwise it's not an environment that people want to live in.'

Building in flexibility

Tigg + Coll had previously completed another student housing project in London, Nido Spitalfields. Designed to feel more like a member's club than a dorm, this project had helped redefine what the typology could be, thanks to a range of facilities not typically found in student accommodation, such as an auditorium and a cinema room. But although it looked impressive, it soon became apparent that it wasn't working as efficiently as it could have. Spaces were too prescriptive in their function, which limited the ways in which they were used. The auditorium, for instance, would regularly host talks and workshops, but it sat vacant most of the time.

The architects realised they needed to make spaces more flexible and ambiguous, empowering residents to find new uses themselves. Chapter King's Cross was designed with this strategy in mind. Rooms come in different shapes and sizes, suitable for a variety of events and activities, but almost all of them double up as casual areas for lounging, socialising or studying. 'It was a more mature approach,' explains Tigg. 'We were more confident in what we were doing and knew that we didn't have to be so formal.'

This is particularly evident in the designated games and events room. Ping-pong tables run down the centre, but most of the time they serve as study desks, with seating provided by leather-upholstered benches. The room is also kitted out with projection equipment, so it can be set up to host talks. 'It works well within the philosophy,' says Tigg. 'For the five times a year they put on special events, things can be moved out quite easily. For the rest of the time, it allows people to study and commune however they want.'

Fig 2.1.1 A games area and events room features ping-pong tables that double as study desks. The space also includes projection equipment, so it can host talks and workshops

Fig 2.1.2 The reception looks like the arrivals hall of a Victorian railway station, helping to reinforce its public nature. Details include a large oak bench and carriage-style seating booths

Creating a public character

The floor plan is organised around a spacious entrance reception, designed in the spirit of an arrivals hall. The reception desk and security gates are located to the rear, rather than at the front, making the majority of this space open to visitors. There are seating booths, lounge spaces and computer workstations, so residents can meet with friends, family and other guests in different ways. The design aesthetic reinforces the public nature of the space, while also referencing the heritage of the location. Much like King's Cross station nearby, it looks like a Victorian railway concourse, with industrial lighting, a large oak waiting bench and a mosaic tile floor. Other details include mailboxes set into wood-panelled walls, textiles based on London Underground fabrics, and bespoke metalwork. These are all materials built to last, not just to look good.

This rich palette of materials and references continues through the communal spaces on the ground and first floors, where spaces offer more varied degrees of privacy. Tigg says he imagined the layout as a scaled-up version of a Victorian house; it doesn't make sense for every room to be a hive of activity, there should also be places where residents feel comfortable enough to kick off their shoes and share more intimate conversations. One way it does this is with lighting; spaces are daylit wherever possible, while a mix of table lamps and suspended lighting offer different moods that can change through the day.

Fig 2.1.3 A study lounge on the first floor includes a kitchen, so students can prepare meals and snacks while they're working

Fig 2.1.4 The gym is located on a glazed mezzanine, rather than in a dark basement, so users can looks down on others as they work out

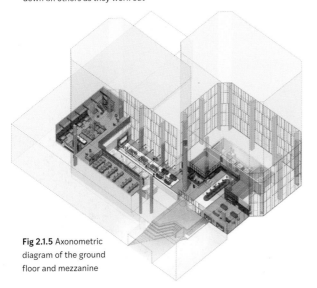

Fig 2.1.5 Axonometric diagram of the ground floor and mezzanine

Sense of life and activity

Views between rooms are another important feature; just because someone needs quiet, it doesn't mean they want to feel isolated. The gym is a good example of this. Instead of being hidden in a dark basement, it can be found on a glazed but sound-insulated mezzanine above the first-floor study lounge. Gym users can look down on others as they work out, while those below can catch a glimpse of activity going on above.

'Buildings aren't dead, they're living things, and we really wanted people to feel that,' explained Tigg. 'After a workout, you might come downstairs to make a smoothie or a cup of tea, and say hello. That kind of soft social engagement is always a nice factor in these buildings.' The lounge also includes a kitchen, so that occupants can prepare meals and snacks at the same time as working or socialising, just as they might do in the kitchen of a private home.

Chapter King's Cross shows that ambiguity is just as important in co-living as it is in a house, that residents need the agency to make spaces their own. The project has become a benchmark for Chapter Living, and Tigg + Coll has since worked on several more of the brand's London sites. Serendipitously, one of these was a reworking of the Nido Spitalfields site. By applying the lessons learned at King's Cross, this location has become every bit as vibrant. Both properties also include a portion of build-to-rent, meaning students actually do have the opportunity to continue co-living after graduation.

Case study: BaseCamp Leipzig

Operator: BaseCamp

Architect: Architekturbüro Irmscher

Interior designer: Studio Aisslinger

Type: Purpose-built student accommodation

Location: Leipzig, Germany

Completion year: 2018

Gross internal floor area: 10,000sqm

BaseCamp offers student housing with a hostel vibe. In Central and Eastern Europe, where high-quality student accommodation is in short supply, the company provides design-led living spaces at affordable prices. Acknowledging that more and more students are travelling abroad to study, its properties prioritise community ahead of luxury, making spaces where young people living away from home for the first time can feel comfortable meeting others. Interiors are bright and busy, but they also have a utilitarian feel.

In Germany, a country that welcomed nearly 400,000 foreign students in 2019, Basecamp's sites include a purpose-built facility in Leipzig.[1] Along with 385 bedrooms, this building contains lounge and study spaces, a coffee bar, a gym, a mini cinema, a party room, communal kitchens, and an outdoor terrace and sun deck. There's approximately two square metres of communal space per resident, so there is plenty of room for everyone to use these facilities, and they are mostly managed by 'Base Buddies' (students employed by BaseCamp) who make sure they operate in a way that best suits the needs and interests of the community.

Based on a boutique hotel

Basecamp chose Studio Aisslinger to design the interiors of all its properties after seeing the studio's design for the 25hours Hotel in Berlin, where industrial materials and street art create a relaxed and informal aesthetic. Basecamp CEO and co-founder Armon Bar-Tur had a vision for student housing that fused the community spirit of American dorms with a European design sensibility, and he felt this approach was the way to achieve it.[2] 'He walked into the studio and said, "I want to do the exact same thing, but for students",' explains Studio Aisslinger's managing director, Dirk Borchering.

Although Basecamp has a mix of both purpose-built and renovated properties, the interiors tend to have a converted-warehouse feel. In Leipzig, concrete walls are left unplastered, wiring and ventilation fixtures are visible on the ceilings, and furnishings are largely made from plywood or steel. These details fit the aesthetic but are also durable long term. 'We don't like fake surfaces,' says Borchering. 'If you scratch them they look really ugly. But natural materials age in a nicer way; if you get a little scratch, it's OK.' To make spaces feel comfortable and lively, these elements are paired with bold flashes of colour, patterned rugs and cushions, and oversized plants.

Room for imagination

Bedrooms come fully furnished, but they don't feel completely finished. Studio Aisslinger found ways to create plenty of storage without filling the rooms with wardrobes and cupboards. 'You need storage

Fig 2.2.1 and 2.2.2 Custom furniture and storage solutions make the bedrooms feel open and adaptable. Elements include underbed drawers, pegboard walls and an extra-long desk

if you're living there for a certain amount of time,' says Borchering, 'but we still wanted to keep the room airy and flexible.' Almost every item of furniture was designed by Studio Aisslinger, either bespoke or for manufacturers. The bed consists of a mattress raised up on a platform, with a wire mesh screen in front and drawers slotted in underneath. A desk runs across the bed platform to create a casual seating area in the corner, while a pegboard wall offers a variety of options for hooks and shelving; it could be a space to store a bicycle, hang coats or display personal objects. Some rooms also have their own kitchenettes, but those without can use shared kitchens dotted through the building.

Fig 2.2.3 Walls are left unplastered to create a raw, industrial aesthetic, but are made to feel more homely with the addition of bright colours, patterned rugs and plants

Fig 2.2.4 The study room features calming shades of pastel pink and green, along with a house-shaped enclosure where small groups can work together

Fig 2.2.5 Playful elements create character in the lounge spaces, including an umpire's chair and cylindrical hut made from corrugated Perspex

The communal areas are organised based on how noisy they are likely to be, with loud spaces at one end and quieter spaces at the other. This creates some unusual relationships; for instance, the laundry room and gym sit alongside the lounge areas. 'They're part of the public space,' says Borchering. 'You start your washing and then you can go and do a workout or chat to a friend while you wait.' Meanwhile the study spaces are more secluded, creating opportunities for focused activities.

Varied colour palettes create distinct identities for each area. Bright blue and pink create a bold look for the reception and coffee bar areas, while the silent study room is coloured in calming shades of pastel pink and green. On the bedroom floors, colour is used as a navigational tool in the corridors, so each storey has its own unique combination of tones and patterns. Even

the laundry room features a vibrant colour palette, with every washing machine given its own identifiable shade.

Studio Aisslinger employed tactics to make spaces feel cosy, even when they are large and open. There are small enclosures – a house-shaped seating booth and a hut made from corrugated Perspex – where groups of students can find privacy. Bookshelves cover entire walls but they aren't filled with stuff, just a few books and plants. Lighting is provided by characterful pendant lights, while metal mesh panels create lower ceilings. There are also some playful elements, like the umpire's chair in the silent study space or the neon signs dotted around the building. Again, almost every element is designed by Studio Aisslinger. 'We try to give every BaseCamp its own story,' says Borchering. 'We want to create something special for every place.'

Case study: The Student Hotel Florence Lavagnini

Operator/Client: The Student Hotel

Architect: Archea Associati

Interior designer: Rizoma Architetture

Type: Student accommodation/hotel hybrid in converted palazzo

Location: Florence, Italy

Completion year: 2018

Gross internal floor area: 21,353sqm

By allowing student residences to double as hotel rooms, The Student Hotel (TSH) has developed a clever design template. The company can offer students premium facilities, flexible rental contracts and the possibility of having family or friends come to stay. When the students aren't there, rooms are rented out to paying guests just like any regular hotel. Not only does this provide financial benefits all round, it creates vibrant communal spaces where students, tourists and locals can intermingle.

In Florence, TSH has applied this concept to a huge 19th-century palazzo. As well as 390 guest rooms, this building now contains co-working and study areas, retail and event spaces, a big communal kitchen and a fully equipped gym. To top it off, the roof has become a lounge deck with a bar, swimming pool and views of the city skyline. As with TSH's other properties, the business is based around an approach that is novel in the

Fig 2.3.1 The ground floor of The Student Hotel Florence is a destination in its own right, with lounge areas, study spaces and shops

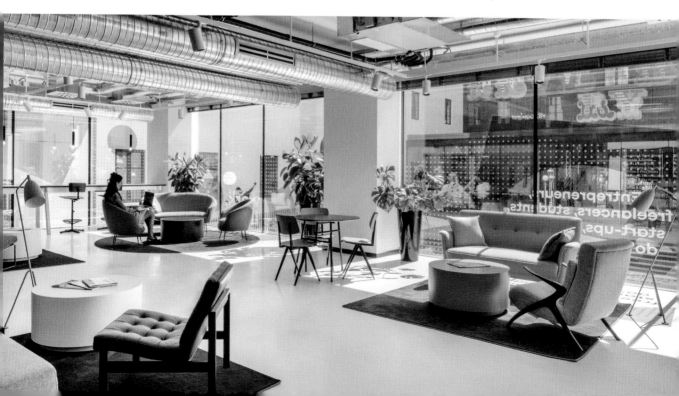

Fig 2.3.2 Communal spaces are organised around a vibrant courtyard, which doubles as a space for art

Fig 2.3.3 The roof is also a big communal space, with a bar, swimming pool and impressive views of the Florence skyline

housing sector – trusting students to behave like adults. Students are given rooms with a superior design quality compared to most dorm rooms, on the understanding that they will be more likely to treat them with respect. 'The housing sector assumes that students are going to destroy a place and steal everything,' says TSH founder and CEO Charlie MacGregor, 'but we've found that if you bring people together in a trustful way and use design to stimulate behaviour, you get a lot of respect and beautiful things happen.'

Combining home and hotel

The hotel function is central to TSH's business model, but also offers the company more flexibility in terms of design. MacGregor, who is originally from Scotland and has a background in property, came up with the concept when he moved to Amsterdam in 2005. At the time, students were protesting on the streets about the lack of viable housing options in the city. To give them the quality, flexibility and affordability they were demanding required a new residential typology. This was difficult to develop within European planning laws, which focus on private rather than shared living spaces, but MacGregor realised he could get around this by instead reinventing the hotel typology, which comes with a different set of planning rules. Bedrooms can be fairly small – more like hotel rooms than apartments – which in turn frees up extra space for communal areas. This means the business can remain viable even when spaces prioritise community-building over profit. It also means that students don't have to sign up for year-long contracts.

'We've built vacancy and flexibility into our model,' MacGregor explains. 'The biggest problem with student housing is that, if you have vacancies in your building, you're in trouble. The weakest point of the student housing model actually became our strongest point; if someone wants to leave a month early, no problem, that's peak season for tourists.'

Bringing people together

A key principle of TSH's model is that students and hotel guests are mixed together, just as they would be in any coffee shop, restaurant or pub. There is an industry-wide reluctance to this, with the perception that it could be dangerous in some way, but MacGregor wants to challenge that. Ground floor areas in particular are designed to become hives of activity. This idea is pushed to the limits in Florence, where around 20% of the building is communal space and the ground floor is a destination in its own right. Lounge and study areas are interspersed with shops, including a record store, a hair salon and a bicycle shop, and arranged around a courtyard dotted with artworks and food trucks. The space regularly hosts events too, from music concerts to lectures and networking events.

Although TSH has its own in-house design team, it often teams up with architecture and design studios. In Florence, the company chose to work with Italian practices Archea Associati and Rizoma Architetture, who helped get the best out of the palazzo's difficult floor plan. The maze of small rooms was opened up where possible and generous amounts of glazing were added, making it easier to see what's happening in a

Fig 2.3.4 Bold colours and slogans add character to the bedrooms, which are designed to suit both students and hotel guests

room next door, even if you can't hear it. 'We like how, if you're in a meeting room, there's something out the window to keep you occupied,' says MacGregor. 'That distraction for us stimulates imagination.' Similar rules apply in the basement, where rooms are more domestic in function. The laundry and games rooms are tactically positioned alongside one another, while the 260sqm kitchen is a single space grouped into eight islands, so that residents can cook with a group of friends but also to chat to neighbours.

A spirit of playfulness

Bold colours and slogans play an important role. In the bedrooms, they offer a measured amount of character – even long-stay guests don't need to dress their rooms, but they can find space for personalisation if they want it. Elsewhere these details add a playful quality, from the wall of 'lost socks' in the laundry room to the bright red music room. The phrase 'The Beach is Boring' emblazons the swimming pool, while the entrance lobby is neon pink and features playground swings. 'Where you see the humour in the design, it makes you smile,' says MacGregor. It was even possible to add signage to the exterior of the historic building, thanks to the support of the city mayor. 'If you want to genuinely preserve a historic monumental building, you should welcome the fact that it's changing,' adds MacGregor. 'If you embrace that change, you give it sustainability for the next generation.'

The Student Hotel now has more than a dozen venues open in cities all over Europe. Although some have questioned its affordability for students, there is no doubt that the model is welcome in a market that a decade ago offered little choice or quality.[3] With more and more European universities offering courses taught in English, the number of students moving abroad to study will probably continue to increase. The opportunity to stay in housing with high design quality and flexible contracts makes this an even more attractive option. MacGregor mentions examples of students who rent a room for most of the year, but spend the rest of their time travelling around the continent, staying in other TSH venues, sometimes with family members in tow. It wouldn't be surprising to see this become the new normal for student living around the world.

Fig 2.3.5 Playfulness and humour play a big role in the interior design. The laundry room is designed to look like a retro launderette, with chequered floor tiles and a wall of 'lost socks'

Case study: The Project at Hoxton

Operator: Host

Client: Blackrock

Architect: Stride Treglown

Interior designer: Naomi Cleaver

Type: Purpose-built student accommodation

Location: London, UK

Completion year: 2019

Gross internal floor area: 7,790sqm

The high cost of study and the pressure to succeed is taking its toll on the mental health of students. More than one in five admit to having a mental health diagnosis, most commonly depression (10.2%) and anxiety disorders (8.4%).[4] These conditions are widely considered to be aggravated by the unique experience of generation Z, the first group of people to have grown up with screen-based technology and social media, making them most at risk of insularity.

The Project at Hoxton is a live, responsive experiment in student living that aims to tackle this problem. This project was designed by Naomi in collaboration with communications agency This Works, and a team of specialist neuroscientists and psychologists including Professor Kate Jeffery of UCL and Professor Gregory Blimling of Rutgers University, and the building aims to enhance health and wellbeing through habitat. Containing 270 rooms for undergraduate students, most of whom are living away from home for the first time, the abiding motif is 'connections': connection between resident students, connections with all senses, connection with new life experiences, and connection with the local community in east London.

Recent studies show the major impact of the undergraduate years is less to do with what goes on inside the classroom and more to do with what goes on outside. It's the friends you make, the peers you have.'

PROFESSOR GREGORY BLIMLING

A caring approach

One of the most radical interventions was less to do with design and more to do with human resources: the designers advocated for a member of staff dedicated to the pastoral care of students, especially as many are living far from the family home and do not have English as a first language. Often, management and even cleaning and maintenance staff take on this role informally, but at The Project a trained member of staff is committed to not only organising regular events but engaging with all students to ensure they feel supported, able to cope and most of all enjoy their student days. Feedback from students, gathered through an ongoing programme of group meetings and supervised by the student 'pilot', is then acted on and shared, where appropriate, to improve the quality of student accommodation throughout the sector.

Space and decor are designed to reinforce this intention. Unfinished Douglas fir cloaks the reception area, informed by the science behind timber finishes lowering the heart rate and the sound-attenuating effect of texture.[5] Lighting is soft here, fragmented in the way that sunlight is dappled through a forest canopy.

Fig 2.4.1 With wood known to lower the heart rate, Douglas fir surrounds the reception area

Fig 2.4.2 Upholstered huts create moments of privacy within the open-plan ground floor

Fig 2.4.3 Mobile screens and games tables, combined with generous storage, create multifunctional amenity spaces in limited space. There's also a DJ booth featuring nearly 2,000 records, supplied by local record shop Love Vinyl

> People who live in spaces that give them a greater sense of control over their exposure to others are more likely to build positive social connections.'
>
> PROFESSOR KATE JEFFERY

Design for discovery

Viewed directly from reception, the main communal space is segmented with full-height sliding pocket doors, preserving scale and multiple amenities while protecting people from feeling overwhelmed. Space is designed to be discovered, slowly and by invitation. Here upholstered 'huts' also offer moments of more peaceful privacy, while scatter cushions on conversation-friendly curved sofas are filled with camomile and lavender flowers that release relaxing essential oils when crushed.

Much of the furniture here is mobile. A kitchen 'breakfast bar' and dining table are on wheels. So too are metal mesh screens and games tables. Students are encouraged to make the space their own. Even surfaces are designed to be customised: cabinet doors are painted in chalkboard paint for this purpose, and an oversized pinboard features student artwork as well as notices.

Furniture is mobile for another purpose; to make space for guests, namely community groups and cultural institutions, such as the nearby Museum of the Home, but also entrepreneurs, who are invited to hold events and talks or run pop-up shops. Capacious storage here allows furniture to be stowed away when not in use.

Fig 2.4.4 Zones can be partitioned with sliding pocket doors and furniture on wheels, making spaces flexible

Fig 2.4.5 The digital-free zone, where phones, laptops, and anything that goes 'beep' or has a screen is banned, creates a pavilion of peace and quiet

Moments of intimacy

More communal space can be found on the upper levels. A study room features bespoke furniture designed to adapt to both individual and group study. Here, curtains can be drawn to create quiet nooks and a 'soundscape' plays in the background, developed by a collaboration between psychologists and musicians especially for The Project to support concentration and learning through subliminal neurological cues.

At the top of the building is an intimate space in which to completely relax – a digital-free zone where phones and laptops are banned, overlooking a lushly planted terrace. But when it's time to exercise the body–mind connection, there's a fully fitted gym on the ground floor, flooded with natural light through curtain walling and punctuated with cheeky, motivational signage that can be appreciated inside and out.

Private studio rooms are designed to promote the same sense of calm confidence; generous noticeboards and open shelving allow students to decorate in their own style against a biophilic palette of sage green and bronze illuminated with ample natural light, while bespoke joinery maximises storage.

The Project at Hoxton proved to be so appealing – tenancy was, unusually, at 100% before opening – that the building was sold by investors shortly thereafter, though it still operates as student accommodation. This has made it impossible to study the outcomes of interventions. Despite that, The Project still stands as a testament to the multiple and modest possibilities in designing shared environments to enrich mental and physical health.

Fig 2.4.6 Biophilic sage green, along with plenty of storage and display space, enables bedrooms to become oases of calm

Fig 2.4.7 Cheeky messages get the energy going in the gym

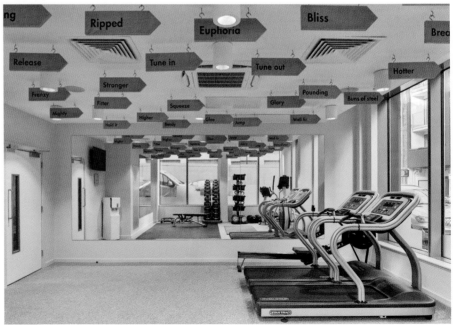

Case study: Calico

Operator: Fresh Student Living

Client: Foundry

Architect: FCH

Interior designer: Naomi Cleaver

Type: Purpose-built student accommodation

Location: Liverpool, UK

Completion year: 2019

Gross internal floor area: 22,176sqm

Calico is one of the largest purpose-built student housing schemes in Europe, providing accommodation for up to 738 students. When asked to design the interiors of this huge project, Naomi realised that the primary challenge would be making it feel homely.

The private living spaces are spacious but cosy, featuring bespoke furniture to maximise storage, and noticeboards and open shelving for personalisation. However, the shared amenity space encompasses 930 square metres – a vast amount of space. A further challenge was that Naomi was brought into the project too late to influence the location of utilities, and for the same reason were obliged to keep the proposal simple and quick to deliver. The key to success was therefore in atomising the space, using largely off-site modular construction and with a playful spirit.

Fig 2.5.1 Tiles give a robust exterior to the various huts that divide up the communal areas

CABIN

Fig 2.5.2 One hut contains a designated selfie booth, embellished with silk flowers

A feeling of control

The solution was to frame both the floor plan and the sections as a loose grid, exploiting column positions and adopting innovative connections with the ceiling to liberate access to power, ultimately creating a 'village' of intimate huts and hideaways that beg to be discovered. The intention was to give to residents what is especially important in a co-live building like this: a feeling of control over the enormous volume they live in, even though it is also shared and rented.

Calico is located in and named for the drapers and milliners, tailors and upholsterers who once flourished in this part of Liverpool. Taking the weave of cloth as inspiration, the huts are faced on the outside in coloured and contrasting tiles and grouts, some sparkling with glitter, to create a palette of highly decorative woven patterns that are still robust and easy to clean in such a busy building.

Inside, walls are faced with sound-absorbent fabric, to compensate for the combination of hard surfaces and volume, in colours to match the tiles. Furniture,

Fig 2.5.3 In the 'co-study' hut, power descends from the ceiling for plug-in desktop power, while thick carpet and upholstered walls soften acoustics

integrated and loose, is in monochromatic shades to intensify the therapeutic effects of the colours selected for the purpose, while planting, inspired by a suit's floral buttonhole, or the corsage on a dress, provides soft detail and biophilic benefit throughout. Planting is particularly dense in one of the huts, where cascades of silk flowers provide a designated selfie booth; one student couple loved this space so much that they got married here.

Signage is conceived with the same care and attention as the rest of the interior. Essential in a building shared by so many, and where few have English as a first language, signage is arguably not redolent of 'home' – but at Calico these sculptural and illuminated signs become decorative objects in and of themselves.

Calico illustrates how large scale needn't be an obstacle to creating the sense of home and community that not only makes people on short-term tenancies want to stay, but to make life-long commitments.

Fig 2.5.4 One of the study areas is a shade of infinite deep blue, to enable greater concentration

Fig 2.5.5 and 2.5.6 There are various game huts, featuring shuffleboard, pool, table tennis and table football. These are clustered away from the study areas, to ensure students here don't disturb others

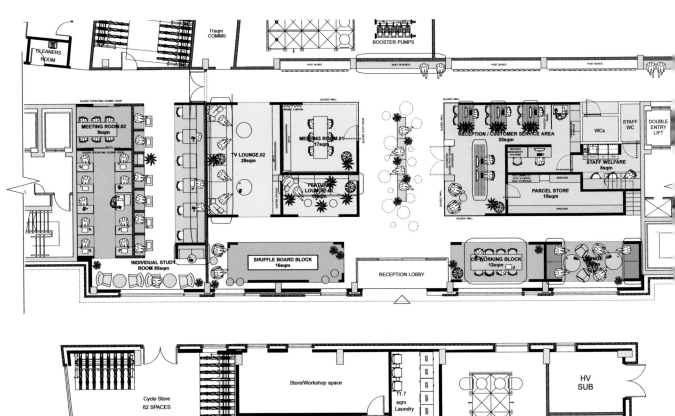

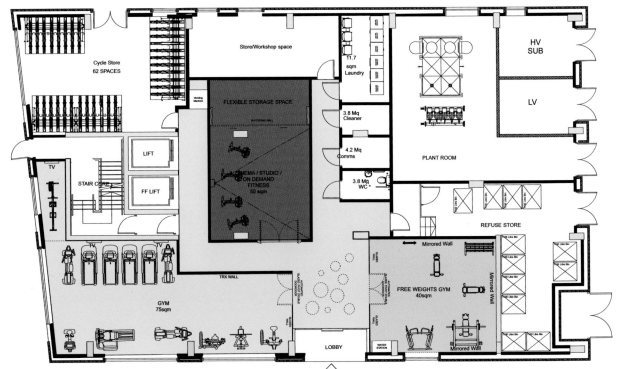

Fig 2.5.7a (opposite above)
Ground floor amenity
space, block A

Fig 2.5.7b (opposite below)
Ground floor amenity
space, block B

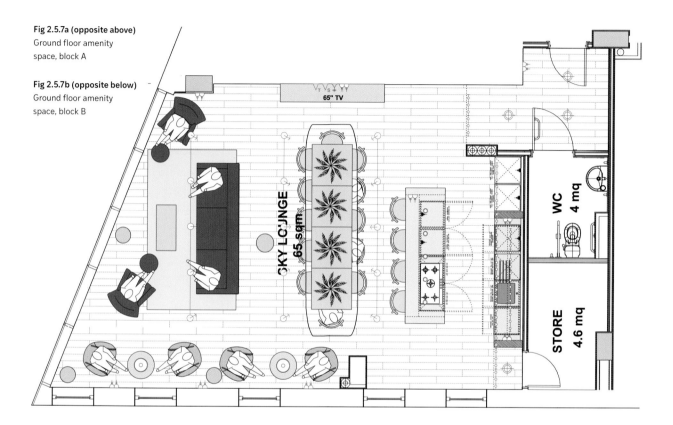

Fig 2.5.7c (above) Sky lounge
floor plan

Fig 3.0.0 Communal living spaces in Cohabs Louise 86, Brussels, 2020

3.
Co-living in the mainstream

Fig 3.0.1 The Collective Old Oak was among the first large-scale co-living communities to offer luxury amenities and services to residents

Living as a service

Back in 2015, it had become clear that student-style accommodation for adults was going to be the next big property market.[1] With PBSA proving successful around the world, shared living had already moved on from being something you put up with while studying, to a style of home with much broader appeal. With design quality and service elements built into the model, there was an obvious attraction for the private rental market, particularly for young adults in the early stages of their careers, not yet ready to buy a home or settle down. It offered them clean, safe and attractive living spaces, in city locations where renters would probably be unable to afford to live on their own.

The term co-living was still in its infancy at that time, although brands like Common, Quarters and Ollie were using it to describe their specific form of shared living, which was gathering pace in cities including New York, San Francisco and Berlin. A cross between student housing and hotels, these developments were relatively straightforward, combining serviced bedrooms with communal lounges, kitchens and (in some cases) bathrooms, and providing everything from toilet paper to shampoo. But it wasn't long before other brands started to up the ante.

Co-working giant WeWork launched its first co-living complex in New York in 2016, combining characterful interiors with the same mix of services and events that had made its workplace model popular. Meanwhile, The Collective opened a co-living development in northwest

London that called itself the world's largest. With millennials as its target, the complex promised residents everything they needed at their fingertips, without them even having to leave the building. As well as 550 en-suite bedrooms and communal kitchens, The Collective Old Oak contains a co-working space, a restaurant, a gym, a spa, a launderette and a cinema. 'Convenience is so important,' said company founder Reza Merchant at the time of launch.[2] 'Nowadays people are just used to everything at a touch of a button. It's essential to provide that same level of convenience and immediacy in the places where people live.'

It's not all about millennials

As it turned out, those in their twenties weren't the only ones interested in this form of shared living. In The Collective's first year, it was observed by community manager Ed Thomas that residents typically fell in two categories: 'early adopters' and those at 'an inflection point in their lives'.[3] The first referred to those with a natural curiosity and willingness to try new things, typically young people but not always. However, the second covered a much more diverse group. They might be graduates moving into their first home

Fig 3.0.2 Designed by AIM Architecture, Cohost West Bund in Shanghai is a co-living community in a converted hotel, offering spacious loft rooms and a distinctive design aesthetic

outside of university, but they could just as easily be thirtysomethings relocating to London for new jobs, or those in their forties or fifties going through divorce or separation. What became clear is that co-living isn't just a radical product for a niche market; it is a model that can be adapted to suit many different kinds of living situations. The Collective's second London location, which is one of our case studies, explores this idea in even greater detail.

With such a diverse audience, co-living developments have naturally also diversified. This period saw the emergence of 'co-living 2.0', a term used to describe co-living buildings that target a slightly older demographic.[4] This typology blurs the boundaries between co-living and build-to-rent, with a package that still centres around shared spaces, but with less emphasis on micro-living and more stylised interiors. It includes

projects like Cohost West Bund in Shanghai, designed by AIM Architecture, which shows how co-living can move beyond a cliched student-style aesthetic and offer more sophisticated, grown-up design. Other co-living developments target specific audiences, like our case study The Italian Building, run by operator Mason & Fifth, which focuses primarily on health and wellness.

Reinventing the shared house

Co-living's service model is increasingly being inserted into existing residential properties too. While it was already common for groups of individuals to share a rented house or apartment, the setup would traditionally be quite informal. But by introducing elements of hospitality, companies like LifeX, Node and Cohabs have shown how large family homes can be organised into high-quality shared living spaces for groups of around

Fig 3.0.3 Targeting young professionals moving to new cities, LifeX offers serviced co-living in Scandinavian-styled apartments. Each property houses between four and eight people

Fig 3.0.4 Cohabs offers large-scale house shares, with many properties containing more than 20 bedrooms. Homes are designed with a focus on upcycled materials and vintage furniture

five to 15 people. Operating more like Airbnb properties than hotels, these homes offer a softer form of co-living that is more suited to introverted characters, for whom the idea of living in a huge complex might seem too daunting. With bedrooms more likely to vary in size, these homes suggest how co-living can more easily cater for couples as well as singles.

The only audience that co-living hasn't yet reached is low-income workers. With the typology still in its early days, most of the current examples come in at the top end of the market – bar a few exceptions, like our case study K9 Coliving. Compared with standard rental properties, the monthly cost of living in one of these properties tends to be significantly more. In some cases, the figure isn't that far off the total monthly earnings of the average UK family. However, once you factor in the additional benefits, the numbers start to make sense. Most of us are used to paying for a whole host of extras out of our earnings – electrical bills, gym memberships, Netflix subscriptions, not to mention household supplies, from kitchen appliances to crockery and bedding. Here, you're looking at one bill that covers all of that, or a big chunk of it at least. But for co-living to become more commonplace, we need more affordable examples to emerge.

Case study: The Collective Canary Wharf

Operator: The Collective

Architect: SOM

Interior designer: The Collective

Type: Purpose-built co-living

Location: London, UK

Completion year: 2019

Gross internal floor area: 21,000sqm

The Collective has built its brand around the idea of 'living as a service'. Tapping into cultural shifts that have led to an increase in mobility and a reduced desire to settle, it positions renting as a lifestyle choice, rather than a fall-back for those unable to afford home ownership. Residents are invited to free themselves from the burden of material possessions, instead having more opportunities for life experiences and personal growth.

At The Collective Canary Wharf, which calls itself the world's largest co-living building, residents have premium facilities at their disposal. The building contains 705 micro-apartments, which are more comparable in size to a hotel room than a one-bedroom flat. Every occupant also has access to amenities that would rarely exist in a private home, including cinema rooms, a 'MasterChef-style' kitchen, gym and exercise spaces, a spa and wellness suite, and a swimming pool that boasts views over London. There's no need to worry about bills or cleaning, and no real difference between staying a night or a year.

Fig 3.1.1 Micro-apartments are fully furnished, with plenty of surfaces and open shelves. The aim is to create spaces where residents can display their own belongings

Fig 3.1.2 Residents have unlimited access to premium facilities, including a swimming pool on the 20th floor, boasting views over London

Fig 3.1.3 A 'MasterChef style' kitchen is divided up into islands so that small groups can comfortably cook together, but the space can also host cooking classes for larger groups

'We're offering people a product that can create a new way of living,' says Thomas Downes, The Collective's head of interiors. Downes believes the model embodies a new shared belief system, that alternative forms of living can improve quality of life. 'There's a huge push against consumer culture,' he explains. 'People understand that there is a strength in being together and a strength in a shared economy.'

Working across scales

While some large-scale co-living developments try to create small neighbourhoods within their buildings, The Collective Canary Wharf treats its residents as a single community, where people are more likely to connect through shared interests than proximity. The theory is that friendships more typically emerge through activities, such as a regular yoga session, than between direct neighbours. The layout of the building reflects this, with shared spaces grouped together instead of split up into clusters.

There are four entirely communal floors: three at the base of the building and another on the 20th storey. These areas are designed to accommodate gatherings, but to also operate at a domestic scale. Examples include the communal kitchen, which is divided up into islands so that small groups can comfortably cook together, but which is also large enough to host a cooking class. The same goes for the library and study; sometimes they host small events, but the rest of the time they offer quiet, cosy corners for reading or studying. This duality is promoted in colour and material choices, which include hardwearing textiles like leather and velvet, warm lighting and shades of green (a colour with proven calming effects).

'Something we're balancing continuously is how we work across various scales,' says Downes. 'We want spaces to be emotionally intelligent so that they can create the best experiences both for individuals and for gatherings.'

Balance purpose with possibility

While this approach allows a degree of flexibility, The Collective tries not to create too much ambiguity. Most spaces can be used for a couple of different functions, but they still have clear purposes, which are signalled through design. The co-working space, for instance, is simple and bright, with white walls, hanging plants and basic furniture. It is not cosy; rather it is an environment suited to focusing on work. 'If you create too much complexity, you start to lose the honesty of what you're trying to do,' explains Downes. 'Spaces either need to do one or two things really well, or be completely open-ended and radical; when you start to live in between you don't execute either particularly well.'

This is also evident in Mthr, the 20th-floor restaurant, where the mood shifts significantly. Cool shades of blue, turquoise and grey combine with high ceilings and sculptural artworks, highlighting this as a space where the emphasis is on hospitality more than homeliness.

Building a sense of belonging

One of the biggest challenges for The Collective's form of co-living is how it gives residents a sense of ownership and familiarity. When over 700 people occupy a building, it can be difficult to maintain a feeling of belonging – even more so when the building doubles as a hotel, offering short stays as well as residences. One

tactic employed here is the use of interactive artworks, including a giant bell that hangs above the entrance lobby, and a metal wire piece dotted with padlocks. These elements, which reference the history of the London Docklands area, are there so that people can subtly make their mark on the building. In the same spirit, corridors are designed as places to linger. The first-floor gallery, for instance, is a welcoming space furnished with curving banquette sofas, low-hanging brass pendant lights and a wall of wooden louvres.

The micro-apartments are also intended to encourage personality, though it may not seem that way. Rooms come in four sizes – cosy, standard, comfy and big – and they are all fully furnished, including bathrooms and kitchenettes. The interiors are certainly not minimalist, with dark joinery and patterned wallpaper, but they include plenty of open shelves and surfaces. Residents are encouraged to display their belongings, even if they don't have many. 'Sometimes people think that offering a pinboard is what's needed to make a space one's own, but I think the objects you own fundamentally contribute to that,' says Downes. The aim of these spaces, he explains, is not to condense the contents of a two-bedroom house, but simply to facilitate the activities you would want to do in private. The rest can take place somewhere else in the building. 'We're pioneering a new future of living, and that means really boiling down the essence of what we need within a space,' he adds.

The Collective is an important experiment into how co-living can operate on a large scale. It demonstrates adaptability – a willingness to evolve based on the

.1.6 In-between spaces like
ntrance lobby and corridors
designed to encourage
ity, with interactive artworks
inviting seating areas

changing demands of the market. It has experimented with short-stay, long-stay and hybrid models, and while it originally targeted students and young professionals, today it looks at a much broader demographic. Even COVID-19 hasn't held the company back; founder Reza Merchant said the spirit of community among residents became stronger during the lockdown period than ever before.[5] 'The fact that members have stayed and are flourishing is proof the model works,' he said. 'I actually think we will look back at this moment in 20 years from now and say that our future as a business was forged during this challenging time.'

Case study: The Italian Building

Operator: Mason & Fifth

Architect: Stiff + Trevillion

Interior designer: Studio Clement

Type: Rented co-living in converted office block

Location: London, UK

Completion year: 2019

Gross internal floor area: 860sqm

Fig 3.2.1 In the lobby, a Murano glass chandelier and terrazzo flooring reference the 'Italian' in the building's name

Wellness is the main focus of co-living brand Mason & Fifth. With its first venue, a converted office block in London's Bermondsey known as The Italian Building, it offers residents a lifestyle centred around fitness classes, creative activities, meditation and healthy eating. Its spaces are designed with the same ethos, with natural materials like cork and linen alongside an abundance of plants. It is an environment designed to target a specific audience, namely those interested in sharing a healthy lifestyle with others.

The Italian Building contains 28 bedroom 'studios', spread over four storeys. With an area of just 16sqm, each of these compact spaces contains a double bed, an en-suite bathroom, and a small kitchenette and dining space. In addition, there's an entire floor assigned to communal activities, with a large living and dining room, a shaded outdoor terrace and a laundry room. Fitness classes, which include yoga, pilates and personal training, take place in a neighbouring building.

A shared sense of purpose

Unlike a lot of other co-living companies, Mason & Fifth includes its programme in the rental package. Residents are free to (and are encouraged to) participate in as many group activities as they like, from fortnightly 'rant and reflect' talking circles to craft workshops and 'family' dinner parties, and they have access to a range of add-ons that include organic toiletries, house bicycles, housekeeping services and a MUBI movies subscription. The only thing that costs extra is food; rather than prepare your own meals, you can opt in to breakfasts, packed lunches and dinners prepared by the in-house chef. The idea is that, by making shared meals and programmed activities part of residents' daily routines, they are likely to forge stronger bonds with one another.

The material aspects of the building's interior are the work of design office Studio Clement, led by Rose Wilkinson and Hannah Birtwistle. With such a specific focus around personal wellbeing, it was important that Mason & Fifth's spaces reflected the brand's message without overdoing it. 'The interior needed to speak about the brand and all the things that they were trying to do,' explains Wilkinson. 'But we didn't want to dominate those spaces, so that you felt like you were literally living in the brand.' They avoided bold slogans and statement design pieces, and instead opted for tactile surfaces, complementary colours, and an emphasis on fresh air and daylight. Unique artworks are dotted through the spaces, and much of the furniture is vintage. 'We were trying to create neutral spaces that had warmth, texture, light, movement and softness – all the words that are encapsulated in the language of the brand,' Wilkinson explains.

Defining different zones

One of the most distinctive spaces in the building is the communal living room, which is designed to accommodate various different activities, often simultaneously. The room is divided up into clusters, which can be made visually private with the use of white curtain partitions. All the furniture is movable, so things can easily be lifted aside when necessary. 'Flexibility was key, because that room is used in so many different ways at different times of the day and week, but we didn't want it to feel like it didn't have purpose,' says Wilkinson. Each zone has its own subtle but distinct character. The group dining area is the most expressive, combining a vibrant shade of green with oversized pendant lights and an oak table. An area for music features an old record player, while a corner table looks suited to work or study. Rugs help to define these various zones, offering warmth at the same time, and headphones are provided so that it's possible to watch a movie or football match without disturbing everyone else in the room.

The bedroom suites come in two layouts; as well as the more typical en-suite rooms, there are also two-level bedrooms where the bed is raised up on a mezzanine above the bathroom. These layouts were developed by architect Stiff + Trevillion, partly in response to the position of the building's windows, but also because there were generously high ceilings on the ground and fourth floors. So while these rooms are around half the size of what is typically permitted in London for a one-bedroom flat, they still manage to offer separate spaces for sleeping, bathing and eating.

Studio Clement's design approach for the bedrooms was to make them feel both neutral and rich at the same time. 'We desperately didn't want these rooms to feel small, yet they are small,' says Wilkinson. Cork was chosen for the floors, offering softness underfoot without dominating in the way that carpet would. The kitchen units are white, matching the walls, with as much open shelving as possible. This means the only standout elements are the speckled granite work surfaces and the occupant's own belongings. Bathrooms are fronted by translucent glass, so that natural light can reach these spaces, while bedsheets and blankets come in a mix of pale shades and simple patterns. 'It was about keeping the focus of detail in special moments, then everything else is blending,' says Wilkinson.

It's all in the details

Many design decisions were influenced by the character and history of the building; for instance, the terrazzo flooring and Murano glass chandelier in the entrance hall reference the 'Italian' in its name. Other elements build on the idea of healthy living. Plants clearly play a big role, with biophilic design studio Ro Co behind the selection of greenery. Wardrobes are made from grasscloth, a material comprising strands of hemp, jute, seagrass and other natural fibres, while joinery was provided by Goldfinger, a company that sources waste wood. There is also a 'tech detox' box in every bedroom, so that residents can stow away their phones at night (helping them to switch off) and instead rely on alarm

Fig 3.2.2 Biophilic design studio Ro Co chose plants for the building, including a large set of planters at the entrance

Fig 3.2.3 The communal living room is divided up into zones, to make it feel more welcoming and homely in scale. White curtains can be used to partition the space when required

clocks for morning wakeup calls. Wilkinson describes this as a process of layering. 'It's always in the little details that the design really comes through and shines.'

Mason & Fifth was only able to create co-living in this location thanks to a planning loophole; because the project is a conversion rather than a newbuild, it was possible for the architects to sidestep regulations relating to minimum space standards. But the fact that The Italian Building wasn't built for purpose is actually one of its greatest strengths. Its elegant windows and generous proportions, combined with its warm and welcoming interior design, have resulted in a building that feels spacious and airy throughout.

The Italian Building was completed shortly before COVID-19 hit the UK, so among its first residents were NHS workers invited to stay in the rooms for free. But going forward, Mason & Fifth is looking to target a diverse audience. The brand believes there are many people in their thirties and fourties, particularly women, who can afford to live alone but would prefer not to, and want something of more quality than a typical flat share. This building has been carefully designed to offer exactly that.

Fig 3.2.4 In the mezzanine studio bedrooms, the bed is raised up above the bathroom, creating a more natural division of space. Colours are kept neutral here, to avoid making the rooms feel too busy

Case study: Vivahouse Soho

Operator/Client: Vivahouse

Architect/Interior designer: Design Haus Liberty

Type: Short-stay rented co-living in disused office

Location: London, UK

Completion year: 2019

A bedroom pod designed to look like a boutique hotel room is at the heart of Vivahouse's co-living concept. These self-contained units can be inserted into any disused commercial building – be it an office or a shop – to turn it into a shared living environment. This gives every resident their own private, lockable bedroom, while the leftover spaces become communal areas. The pods may be small, but they are well made and thoughtfully designed, with attractive furnishings and plenty of storage. They offer an urban living solution that can be more affordable than the fully serviced co-living model, but with more facilities than a typical shared flat or house.

The first Vivahouse property, and the pilot project for the bedroom pods, was a disused office on the second floor of a building next to Tottenham Court Road station in central London. For a year, the building was temporarily transformed into a shared home for three people. Three bedroom pods were installed, each with soundproof walls and its own digital locking system, while the rest of the space became living areas, with an open-plan kitchen, dining room and lounge, and two shared bathrooms. It wasn't hugely radical, but it identified an important gap in the market – people who are new to a city or only staying for a limited time. These individuals are understood to be less concerned with the size of their space than the quality of lifestyle that it offers, whether that means meeting new people, a premium location or being able to find sanctuary after a hectic day.

Although Vivahouse Soho wasn't a cheap place to live (rent was £1,800 per month), it offered residents all these things. Rental contracts were flexible, bedsheets were provided, cleaning and laundry services were included, and every resident was given unlimited access to co-working facilities in the same building. Plus, all the attractions of London's West End were within walking distance.

Learning from WeWork

Vivahouse is a partnership between entrepreneur Rajdeep Gahir and architect Dara Huang. Gahir was formerly head of sales for WeWork and led the co-working giant's expansion into Europe. Her vision was to take the WeWork business model (upgrading existing properties by integrating technology and services) and apply it to the residential sector. But unlike WeLive, the brand's own venture into co-living, Gahir wanted a model that would be viable for stays of longer than a few weeks, without compromising on design quality or opportunities for social interaction. 'WeLive has the coolest co-living sites, but the price point is crazy high,' she explains. 'There's a great vibe, but it only really works as a hotel.' Vivahouse makes the model more efficient with the use of prefabricated construction. The bedroom pods, designed by Huang, were developed with mass production in mind. Made from structural insulated panels (SIPs), these high-quality units can be produced at cost, flat-packed for easy storage, adapted to fit different locations and customised to suit the preferences of a landlord or an occupant.

The Vivahouse concept also draws on Huang's own experience with co-living. Her studio, Design Haus Liberty, previously created the interiors for The Collective Old Oak. The client's brief had been to tailor the design to students, but the company later decided to target a wider demographic. Huang now feels the design is mismatched to its occupants. With Vivahouse, she wanted to show how co-living can cater for a broader audience, with more of a luxury design feel. 'I had the idea to create very sophisticated interiors, but in an ageless and inexpensive way,' Huang explains. 'There's a real stigma around co-living; you automatically think you have to be a student or a young person to live there, but you could be 40 years old and single. You shouldn't have to feel ashamed about it.'

A self-contained bedroom

The prototype pods, which were installed at the Soho space, measure 10.5m long and 8.5m wide. Inside, the layout makes optimum use of space without the need for too many bespoke elements, so there is a mix of off-the-shelf furnishings and custom joinery. A double bed is framed by a wardrobe and overhead cupboards, offering plenty of storage space. A chest of drawers and mirror form a dressing area, while a simple shelf can be used as a desk.

While each pod is the same in layout, the finish can be completely different. Unlike a lot of prefabricated rooms designed by architects, these bedrooms are designed to be as comfortable as possible, with both hard and soft furnishings, and plenty of colours and textiles in the mix. The three pods that were installed at Vivahouse Soho feature grown-up shades of deep blue, rusty red and soft grey. These are complemented by matching bedsheets, rugs, bedside tables, lighting and framed artworks, along with shelves and surfaces that residents can personalise with their own belongings. 'We wanted to make a miniaturised hotel room, so that even though it's really small, it's really comfortable,' explains Huang. Other details help to add a feeling of quality, from lighting integrated into joinery to plug sockets with USB ports. Different headboards and cabinet handles were also selected for each space. 'They look bespoke and that is a real differentiating factor,' adds Gahir.

Planning for change

In the shared spaces at Soho, the interior design reflected the temporary nature of the co-living setup without being low quality. Built-in features like the kitchen were cheap and cheerful, but they were accompanied by classic furniture pieces that could look good in any setting. Plants were also dotted through the space. 'The whole idea was to buy durable things that are good quality, with the idea that you can move them,' explains Gahir. 'We have a whole process, together with the pods and partitioning systems, where everything is taken out, put in storage and redeployed later.'

Fig 3.3.1 Capable of being installed in any commercial building, Vivahouse's prefabricated bedrooms are constructed using a panel-based system that can be flatpacked

Fig 3.3.2 and 3.3.3 Designed to look like boutique hotel rooms, the bedrooms have a grown-up aesthetic, with distinct colour palettes and quality textiles

Fig 3.3.4 Communal spaces at Vivahouse Soho were furnished with items that could be easily moved to new locations, including classic furniture pieces and large plants

Fig 3.3.5 Access to both the building and the bedroom pods was managed with keyless digital locking systems, accessed via fingerprint or mobile phone

The Vivahouse model faces a big hurdle when it comes to planning regulations. Gahir's vision was to scale up the Soho project, creating larger and more permanent co-living spaces in various disused commercial buildings around London, such as the closed-down Whiteleys shopping centre where the company held its launch party. But while it was easy to gain planning permission for Soho, the same rules don't apply elsewhere. In that case, Vivahouse was granted a temporary change of use before the building was redeveloped. To achieve change-of-use permissions on a long-term basis is much more challenging, without either a change in planning laws or the support of the government. So for now, the company is looking at more traditional rental models and exploring alternative uses for its flatpack pods. In any case, Vivahouse's approach offers a new perspective on the role prefabrication can play in creating shared living environments.

Case study: K9 Coliving

Operator: Private landlord (formerly Tech Farm)

Interior designer: Tech Farm

Type: Rented co-living in converted hotel

Location: Stockholm, Sweden

Completion year: 2016

Gross internal floor area: 1,100sqm

This former hotel in Stockholm is home to a co-living community of more than 50 people. What were once guest rooms are now residential bedrooms, while the old reception and restaurant spaces have been transformed into communal living and co-working spaces. But unlike other rental conversions of this scale and type, K9 Coliving is run by its residents, not a company. After the real-estate startup that founded the project collapsed and the building was bought by an investor, tenants took charge. It is a shared home that has been shaped more by habitual use than by design, and which continues to evolve as occupants figure out what does and doesn't work. What it may lack in design vision, it makes up for in community spirit and a DIY attitude.

A process of co-creation

K9 has its founders to thank for its autonomous structure. It was initially set up and managed by Tech Farm, a company founded by entrepreneurs Lisa Renander

Fig 3.4.1 A former hotel conference room is now used as a co-working space by residents, but also includes a home cinema area and a greenhouse space where residents play chess

and Fredrik Forss. Their approach differed from the serviced apartment model of co-living, in that they saw themselves as community facilitators rather than operators. The idea was always to empower residents to self-manage their home environment and make it their own. So when Tech Farm went out of business, K9 was already self-sufficient.

The interior design was developed in the same spirit. Renander and Forss initially consulted with designers, but ended up taking a more collaborative approach. They hired a project manager, Helene Gammelgaard, who embarked on a process of 'co-creation' with the first cohort of residents they had selected. As many of these people worked in the creative industries (a deliberate move by the founders) Gammelgaard found they had plenty of expertise in-house. She would host meeting nights where the group would brainstorm ideas. 'We were flooded with great ideas coming from the ground up,' she explains. 'It was a wonderfully inspiring process.' The project took just six months from start to finish, although some people moved in before completion, meaning they could test ideas as they went along. This helped to instil a sense of ownership in the community from the very start. 'It was both a hurdle and a blessing in disguise,' says Gammelgaard.

A converted hotel

The generous floor plan of the former hotel provides a diverse mix of spaces. As well as single and double bedrooms, there are dorm rooms and 'sleeping pods'. There are five different kitchens in total, ranging from the big and sociable to the quiet and intimate. There's even a 'zen room', used for mindful activities such as yoga and meditation.

Some of the former hotel facilities take on a similar role in the co-living setup. The reception, for instance, is still primarily an entrance space, albeit one with a more domestic character. There is a kitchen where occupants can conveniently make a cup of coffee for guests, and a cloakroom where everyone stores their coats and boots. Other areas are completely unrecognisable from before, like the gym that occupies the former hotel closet. Every space is designed to be as useful as possible.

K9 resident Jonathan Andersson says the versatility of the interior is one of the building's biggest successes. 'The layout of the place is amazing when it comes to co-living,' he explains. 'Many of the furnishings are flexible, which gives us the opportunity to change things around.' He points to a former conference room on the first floor as an example. This room mostly functions as a co-working space, furnished with long tables and assorted chairs, but also includes a greenhouse area that is intermittently used for playing music or chess. In the evenings, a lounge area allows the room to turn into a home cinema. It can also be reconfigured to host parties and events – the greenhouse walls are on castors and held in place by simple locks, making them easy to move in and out.

Consensus decision-making

Although K9's spaces are often changing, the decisions that shape them are not taken lightly. To ensure the

Fig 3.4.2 The greenhouse walls are on castors and held in place by simple locks, so it is easy to move them when residents want to use the room for other activities

Fig 3.4.3 A 'zen room' is used for mindful activities such as yoga and meditation

satisfaction of everyone, not just the majority, proposals for home upgrades and group activities are put to a vote and only actioned if a consensus is reached. 'If one person doesn't feel safe with something, or say they can't live with it, then we don't do it,' explains Andersson. 'It's the most important principle we have.' The landlord also plays a role in keeping the household running smoothly, not only by taking care of household cleaning and repairs (a common source of friction in shared houses), but also by assigning a monthly budget towards new ideas and projects. This incentivises more people to take an active role in planning the future of their home.

K9 Coliving proves that, while organisation is key to creating functional co-living communities, it doesn't have to come from the top down. In this case, giving power to residents from the outset was fundamental in securing the long-term future of their shared home.

On a recent visit, Gammelgaard noticed that many of her original furniture purchases had been moved around the building or swapped for residents' own belongings. It's a sign that the building is treated like a home, rather than a museum. 'It's a bit more cluttered now,' she adds, 'but a lot more homely.'

Case study: LifeX Classen

Operator: LifeX

Interior designer: LifeX

Type: Rented co-living in five-bedroom apartment

Location: Copenhagen, Denmark

Completion year: 2018

Gross internal floor area: 229sqm

The shared house is a form of co-living that many people will have experienced at some point in their lives, most likely in the years between leaving the parental home and settling down with a partner. Although it is a common arrangement, very few properties are actually set up to be used in this way, either in the financial model or the design. Groups of individuals will occupy homes designed for families, where they have to navigate the politics of joint contracts and shared furniture. Things inevitably become tricky when some bedrooms are bigger than others or when one person wants to move out early.

What LifeX has done is combine the shared home with a service model, taking all the hassle out of the process. The co-living company manages over 50 houses and apartments in six European cities, which mostly accommodate between four and eight people. Designed to make sharing easy, every home is kitted out with chic Danish furniture and essential household supplies, and tenants have personal, flexible contracts based on the specifics of their rooms. There are spaces on offer for singles and couples, and opportunities to move between properties. Rather than stop-gap homes for young

Fig 3.5.1 Classen's living space is designed to be both comfortable and versatile, with furniture that divides the space into two distinct zones

people, these are aspirational living spaces for people of all ages. They look like homes people settle down in, yet they are designed around a model of flexibility, mobility and sociability.

Settling into a new city

LifeX founders Sune Theodorsen and Ritu Jain initially set up the business as a residential solution for themselves, inspired by their own experiences of living and working abroad. Theodorsen grew up in Denmark while Jain is from India, but they met while working together in San Francisco. They both found the move to a new city made easier by having a supportive network of colleagues around them, so when the couple decided to move to Copenhagen, they devised a way to apply the formula to a living situation. They found a six-bedroom apartment, furnished it themselves, then rented out the extra rooms to other people who were new to the city. Not only did this create an instant network of friends around them, it gave them a level of design quality they wouldn't otherwise have been able to afford. The demand was greater than they were expecting, proving there was a huge market of people moving around internationally for short periods of time. It was the incentive they needed to turn the idea into a business. 'That model of buying a house and living in it for 30 years doesn't work in a world where things change so quickly,' says Theodorsen.

Scandinavian sensibility

A defining quality of LifeX homes is a modern Scandinavian aesthetic, achieved through a partnership with Danish homeware brand Hay. LifeX has an in-house design team that plans the layout of each home, then selects products that best fit the arrangement of the spaces and the number of occupants they will accommodate. Hay then delivers all of the furnishings in a single shipment, making it an efficient and cost-effective process. This includes large furniture items like sofas and beds, but also decorative accessories and functional items like kitchenware. 'One of the nice things about sharing is that you can invest a bit more in the interior design,' says Theodorsen. 'We want every home to be a place that Ritu and I would want to move into.'

The design team has learned through experience which products work best in terms of both popularity and durability. According to LifeX's head of design, Mikkel Krøijer, the aim is to make homes feel simple and uncluttered. They aren't afraid of statement pieces, but they try to pick timeless designs rather than following trends. 'Our design philosophy is very rooted in the Nordic traditions of focusing on doing the basics really well,' Krøijer says. 'We want our members to feel at home, so our interiors must reflect the people that live in them and make them feel that they can be themselves.'

In Classen, one of the Copenhagen properties, furniture plays a key role in defining the layout. The home is centred around a large living space, divided into two zones. On one side, a long narrow dining table offers enough room for all residents to sit down and eat together. On the other, a large L-shaped sofa and armchair create plenty of lounge space. Other details – a dark blue rug, a freestanding shelving unit, side tables and a variety of lighting elements – make the space feel comfortable and versatile.

Bedrooms are designed with the same level of care as the living spaces. They come in various sizes, but most include a desk and a seating area so occupants can use the spaces for other activities besides sleeping. Rooms are assigned to either singles or couples based on a number of factors – not only the size of the room, but also the amount of storage available and the total number of occupants in the property. 'Getting the ratio of people right is one of the core things to creating a healthy community,' suggests Theodorsen. Colour also plays an important role – objects, cushions and blankets in vibrant shades make spaces feel lively, without imposing too much personality.

Familiarity and individuality

Extra character is created with the addition of plants, ceramics and framed artworks. These often include references to local history and culture; for instance, Classen and some of the other Copenhagen homes feature graphic posters on the walls, while London homes display scientific illustrations of animals and plants. The idea is for every property to have an identity that fits its setting, but to also be recognisable as part of the LifeX family. This familiarity is important; it means if a resident's circumstances change, say they want to move in with a partner or they get a new job elsewhere in the city, moving to another LifeX property

Fig 3.5.2 As well as furniture, LifeX homes are furnished with objects, plants, artworks and accessories, so they feel homely right away

is an attractive option. It also means that someone can visit a foreign city and enjoy the same comforts they do at home, by simply organising a 'weekend swap' with another resident.

LifeX shows that it's possible to enjoy more mobile lifestyles without switching to an entirely new form of home. In the same way that Airbnb has created a more homely alternative to the hotel, these properties offer a counterpoint to the large-scale co-living of brands like The Collective and WeLive. It may not offer all the same luxuries, but it allows residents to hold on to some domestic comforts. This, combined with the flexibility for couples, means that LifeX homes can attract a more diverse range of residents than other co-living setups. With young professionals living alongside empty-nesters and retirees, these are multigenerational homes without any families involved. And there is also the option to easily swap properties if you and your adopted 'family' don't get along.

'I think there is still value in coming home to something that looks and feels like a normal home,' adds Theodorsen. 'One of the key qualities of LifeX is that it's not a dorm. People like to come home to something that feels like normal family life, just with a different group of people.'

Fig 3.5.3 Bedrooms usually include a desk space and a seating area, so residents can easily spend time away from their housemates when they choose to

Fig 3.5.4 Kitchens are smart and clean, and fully equipped with crockery, utilities and basic supplies like olive oil, sugar and spices

Case study: Flatmates

Operator: Station F

Client: Station F/Xavier Niel

Architect: Wilmotte & Associés

Interior designer: Cutwork

Type: Purpose-built co-living

Location: Paris, France

Completion year: 2019

Gross internal floor area: 12,000sqm

With the arrival of Station F, the world's largest accelerator campus, Paris has become a new hotspot of emerging talent. Containing more than 1,000 tech startups and creative businesses, this converted freight train depot has transformed the work scene in the French capital, cultivating a new culture of entrepreneurship and co-working. To accommodate the new arrivals this inevitably brings to the city, investor Xavier Niel gave architecture studios Wilmotte & Associés and Cutwork the task of designing an equally innovative residential development. Their response was to create a hybrid co-living model, where some living spaces are shared by everyone, while others belong to small groups.

Comprising three towers, the Flatmates complex provides accommodation for up to 600 residents. Everyone has access to certain amenities, including a cafe, a lounge bar and a large events hall, but the majority of the living spaces come in the form of apartments that are each shared by six residents. What makes these apartments unusual is that they are specifically designed to allow people who don't know

Fig 3.6.1 Flatmates is made up of six-person apartments that are designed to make sharing easier. They include large, flexible living spaces that can be used for various purposes

one another to easily cohabit. First, the management team uses a tech platform called Whoomies to match personality types, to increase the chances that flatmates will get along with each other. Second, bedrooms are suitably private, and there are enough bathrooms to ensure that residents either have an en-suite to themselves or share with just one other person. Third, living spaces are designed to be open and flexible, filled with custom-designed furniture that allows them to adapt to a range of group dynamics and situations, sometimes simultaneously.

Providing privacy and sociability

Cutwork developed the interior design concept around the understanding that people need opportunities for both sociability and privacy in their homes. 'The idea of co-living is about living in a place that is designed for interaction,' explains Cutwork co-founder Antonin Yuji Maeno, 'but it's only possible to live together if there is always the possibility to be alone. The configuration of the space needs to allow people to be away from each other, as well as to interact.'

Maeno used a Japanese interpretation of space to create three different modes for the Flatmates living rooms. In the Japanese language, there are three words for space, all with different definitions: *wa* relates to harmony in a social group, *ba* describes a place where something happens, and *ma* is used for a space in between things. The aim here was to facilitate all three versions, with spaces for focus and introspection, spaces for activity and collaboration, and also spaces

Fig 3.6.2 Each flat features a modular sofa made up of six upholstered seats and three backrest cushions, able to be arranged in multiple configurations

that allow for spontaneous encounters and the unexpected. The architect believes that all three are required to create environments where residents can feel comfortable at all times.

'The big question we were asked was, what is a living room in a co-living space?' says Maeno. 'For us, it is clearly not the same as a traditional family apartment living room. You won't have a sofa facing a TV; that doesn't make sense in a space where people are coming and going all the time, and different personalities want to do different things in different moments.'

Fig 3.6.3 As well as more traditional seating arrangements, it's possible to arrange the sofa modules to create different zones. This means that various activities can take place simultaneously

Fig 3.6.4 Cutwork created 15 custom furniture designs for the apartments, including a dining table with benches and stools, as well as multiuse side tables and storage shelves

New types of furniture

With this in mind, Cutwork developed 15 pieces of furniture that would allow spaces to take on multiple different layouts. The most important of these is a modular sofa made up of nine separate elements – six upholstered seats and three backrest cushions. Accompanied by various side tables, these elements offer endless possibilities. They can be made to function like traditional sofas or armchairs; they can be combined to create one huge bed-like seat; they can even be used to create seating islands where people can read or work at a laptop, away from other activities taking place in the room.

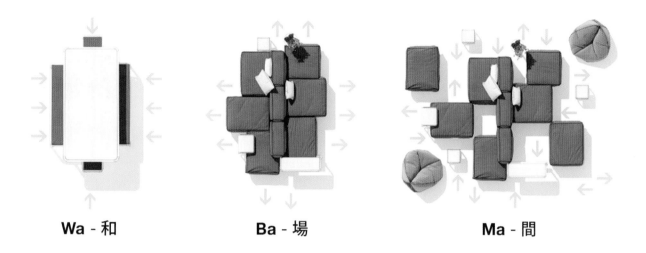

Wa - 和   **Ba** - 場   **Ma** - 間

In the same spirit, the dining table comes with benches and stools rather than traditional dining chairs, so that these pieces can take on different uses at other times of the day. Made from bendable steel tubes, every piece is lightweight enough to be easily moved. So far, the concept seems to be working – building operators report that most residents tend to change the layouts every two or weeks, to support different activities.

A new way of living

Flatmates is among a number of co-living and co-working spaces that Cutwork has worked on. Maeno and co-founder Kelsea Crawford set up the studio specifically to explore the new ways that people are living and working together. This project is mostly targeting young people in their twenties and thirties, particularly those who are living in Paris for the first time. The majority of bedrooms are for singles, although

Fig 3.6.5 The concept is based on the three different Japanese words for space, which all suggest slightly different types of mood and situation

it's also possible to sign up for a 'loverz package' for couples. However, Cutwork is also (through another project) exploring how co-living spaces can be designed for more multigenerational living, finding synergies between people of different age groups.

Maeno believes that shared living is very much in its infancy, and that even more design models will emerge as the typology continues to gain pace. 'We have built all our cities around this standard model, of the modern nuclear family, but it's not the standard any more,' says Maeno. 'The way we live has changed, the way we work has changed. We founded Cutwork because we believe there needs to be a new way to design and to think about space for these new standards.'

Fig 4.0.0 Shared garden at
Lange Eng, Copenhagen,
by Dorte Mandrup
Arkitekter, 2009

4.
Generations come together

Fig 4.0.1 Designed by Mole Architects, Marmalade Lane in Cambridge shows how co-housing communities can offer families a diverse mix of private and social spaces

Shared living works for families

Household formation has undergone rapid change over the past two decades. Thanks to a mix of financial pressures and changing lifestyles, not to mention ageing populations, we've seen household types diversify massively. Single-person homes continue to rise, but the pace has slowed down.[1] Meanwhile, we're experiencing a rise in alternative family models and intergenerational households. The nuclear family is no longer the norm and more varieties of lone-parent households, blended families and non-family households have gained ground. At the same time, different generations are increasingly choosing to live together; young adults are staying in the parental home beyond the age of 30, often for reasons of affordability, while older people are increasingly exploring alternatives to the isolation of self-contained retirement communities.[2]

New models of shared living are needed to facilitate this changing residential landscape. While co-living developments typically only cater for individuals or couples, the ideas that have shaped this typology can just as easily be applied to family and multifamily housing. Unfortunately, the market has been slow in responding to these trends. We have seen the emergence of the build-to-rent model – with projects like the Naomi Cleaver-designed Angel Gardens, which is one of case studies – but the concept is largely not being marketed at families. Meanwhile housebuilders continue to focus on providing homes for a family model that is growing more and more scarce.

This is something that Mole Architects' founder, Meredith Bowles, has learned from experience. 'Once I started getting involved in housing, I realised how poverty-stricken the industry is in terms of ideas,' he explains. 'The vast majority of it is provided by housebuilders who see houses as a product, rather than part of a city or a community.'

Mole Architects was part of the team responsible for delivering Marmalade Lane, a pioneering co-housing project for the UK. It follows a growing trend across Europe for neighbourhoods created and managed by their residents, including our case studies Lange Eng and New Ground. They don't use the term co-living, but the models have plenty in common. These communities consist of groups of individual homes, in various forms, but they also include shared amenities. Usually they'll have a 'common house', which can be a space for socialising, sharing meals and group activities such as exercise, games and art projects. Other shared facilities can include gardens, workspaces, laundry rooms and accommodation for guests. This in turn allows the individual homes to be more space-efficient, making them a more viable option for young couples and retirees, as well as families.

'Looking at examples of how people build houses and live together in Scandinavia and the Netherlands, you see the quality of life they are able to have,' says Bowles. 'In the UK, we have a cultural attitude which is perhaps informed by the kind of places we've all become used to living in – suburban developments. That's perhaps generated a particular attitude towards what we share and what we consider to be importantly or exclusively ours.' The time to change that attitude, it seems, is now.

Making homes multigenerational

Another response to the change in household typologies has been the emergence of a new breed of intergenerational homes. While in the past the so-called 'granny annex' was the only solution on offer, new homes are being developed where multiple occupancy is considered from the outset, allowing them to adapt to a wider variety of changes in family dynamic. As shown by our case studies 3 Generation House and Caring Wood, these homes are typically designed to be separated into two or more self-contained dwellings, which is achieved through clever use of devices such as multiple entrances, flexible partitions and multipurpose spaces. In order for them to function effectively, these homes must also provide a clear distinction between different areas, to ensure that no residents feel their privacy is being compromised.

For many multigenerational homes, the extra living spaces are designed to accommodate older family members, or are for the use of grown-up children who want to live at home with a degree of independence, perhaps while studying or saving for their own properties. But there are other possibilities too. During the COVID-19 lockdown period, stories emerged of these spaces being converted into temporary workspaces and classrooms. Some used theirs to allow at-risk family members to isolate themselves from other residents. When they are not occupied, there's also the possibility of letting them out for short- or long-stay rentals. Providing they have their own entrance, they can help families bring in extra income without impacting

privacy. Ultimately these types of spaces allow homes to be far more versatile than those that simply have extra bedrooms, making it easier for families to handle whatever life throws at them.

Developing new models

Co-living, co-housing and multigenerational homes all become important when dealing with the issues thrown up by our ageing population. Despite living in a society where most other forms of segregation are rejected, our current housing options still separate older people from everyone else, whether in retirement communities or care homes. It doesn't matter if you are in your sixties or your nineties, anyone above retirement age faces the prospect of being cut off from social support structures and stripped of a sense of purpose. This is not appropriate, nor is it viable. Globally, the number of people aged 60 years or over doubled between 1980 and 2017, from 382 million to 962 million. That figure is projected to double again by 2050, exceeding two billion.[3]

The only sensible solution is to find ways of integrating seniors into multigenerational communities. Planned correctly, they can create better living situations for everyone involved. Older residents can share life experiences with younger residents, offering them advice and mentorship that can stay with them as they progress into old age themselves. They can also help out in practical ways, with childcare being the most obvious one. Meanwhile younger residents can offer support with new technologies and trends, helping to keep their elderly neighbours engaged with the world around

Fig 4.0.2 Vikki's Place is a house in New South Wales, Australia, designed by Curious Practice. It incorporates split levels and rolling blinds, so that the owner can partition off sections of the living space for her grown-up son and his family, who often come to stay for long periods

them. 'Living in a complete section of society allows us to stay grounded, fosters heightened respect, and instils a sense of caring,' says architect Matthias Hollwich, a key advocate for intergenerational living.

Hollwich believes multigenerational co-living and co-housing will naturally become widespread, because the baby-boomer generation will be less willing to live in segregation. This is especially the case with the introduction of the sharing economy; it has become easier than ever to connect with people and services, and there's no reason why healthcare systems can't work in the same way. 'Segregating old people in specialised housing is not just inhuman, it is quite dangerous,' he argues. 'Today's system of retirement communities, assisted living facilities and nursing homes is not based on the needs and desires of the older generation, but is instead a commercial solution for ageing that is good business. It lacks the purpose of providing a dignified, self-determined, socially integrated life; 95% of older people want to age at home, yet few can because we do not provide viable solutions.'

While many of these ideas are still being developed, there are already some successful examples of integrated living for seniors. Innovative care homes like our case study Humanitas Deventer offer free accommodation to students, demonstrating how young and old can support one another both emotionally and financially. Innovative property developer Pegasus has teamed up with leading architects to create retirement living in the heart of towns and cities, allowing those over 50 to downsize from their family homes without cutting themselves off from their communities. We are also seeing the emergence of new multigenerational neighbourhoods and agrihoods, like our case study Serenbe, designed to allow people of all ages to live in harmony. One recent concept takes this idea even further: The Urban Village Project, by EFFEKT Architects and Space10, imagines an entirely subscription-based neighbourhood, where residents can move between homes as their needs change, and everyone has access to a range of support and services.

Together, these pioneering projects point to a future where ageing is no longer something to be afraid of.

Fig 4.0.3 and 4.0.4 The Urban Village Project, by EFFEKT Architects and Space10, is a concept for subscription-based housing, with the aim of making cities more livable, sustainable and affordable

Case study: 3 Generation House

Client: Auguste van Oppen

Architect/Interior designer: BETA

Type: Owner-occupied residence divided into two units

Location: Amsterdam, the Netherlands

Completion year: 2018

Gross internal floor area: 450sqm

This five-storey house in Amsterdam allows three generations of one family to live together in a multitude of different ways. 3 Generation House contains a mix of spaces that can be tailored to family members of all ages, from children progressing into adulthood, to grandparents who still have active lifestyles. The building is currently divided into two households – one for a couple and their two children, and another for the maternal grandparents – but it could easily be turned into a single residence, or further subdivided to create an extra two units. It is a home designed to adapt to whatever life brings, however unpredictable.

The affordable option

The house was designed and built by Auguste van Oppen, co-founder of architecture office BETA, for his own family. At first the concept was based solely around the financial benefits of shared living. With property prices in Amsterdam constantly on the rise, it had become impossible for he and his wife, Jantien Oving, to find an affordable family-sized home within the city, so the architect started exploring ways of getting more for less. An idea to redevelop an old monastery into a series of homes didn't work out, but it caught

the attention of Oving's parents, who were themselves looking to move closer to urban conveniences. It got them talking about the other mutual benefits of living together, beyond the cost saving, for things like running errands and babysitting. So when a series of self-build plots became available in Buiksloterham, they decided to give it a try.

Van Oppen designed a five-storey building that splits very easily into two separate homes. The first, for the young family, comprises the two lower floors, half the middle floor, and the garden. The second, for the grandparents, includes the other half of the middle floor, the two upper levels, and a roof terrace looking out over the garden towards the city skyline.

Separate but connected homes

Privacy is created by the way these two residences fit together. Both use the same stairwell, yet access isn't shared. Thanks to a pair of interlocking staircases, each household has its own private route between floors. Cleverly laced together, these space-efficient 'scissor stairs' – more typically found in office buildings than residential – allow both couples to enjoy multilevel living, without having to worry about bumping into each other on the stairs.

'With intergenerational living, it is important to design everything around privacy,' explains van Oppen. 'Many people think this is just one big house, where I'll walk into the kitchen and then my mother-in-law will barge in and be standing next to me. That's not the case; these really are two separate homes.' This difference

Fig 4.1.1 The building contains a home for a couple with two children on the lower levels, and a separate home for the maternal grandparents on the uppermost floors

Fig 4.1.2 and 4.1.3 A pair of interlocking staircases gives each home its own private access route between floors. Called scissor stairs, they also allow the building to take on different configurations

is critical. It means that face-to-face interactions between the two households tend to happen a few times a week, rather than a few times a day, and conversations take place over WhatsApp rather than in the corridors. Yet there are still plenty of opportunities for reciprocal activity. 'Whenever we go to the store, we ask my parents-in-law if there's something they need,' says van Oppen, 'or if we have something come up last minute, we ask them to look after the kids. It makes all of our lives a lot easier.'

Five different configurations

The scissor stairs also give the house its versatility, allowing it to be split in various ways, to take on other configurations. Van Oppen counts five alternative options, all relating to different future scenarios. The first shows how the building will change when the grandparents become older and less mobile. In this scenario, the older couple give up their guest bedrooms on the second floor and live solely on the two uppermost levels, both of which have been designed

Fig 4.1.4 Industrial materials create a practical and durable interior, able to withstand regular activity. Walls are exposed breeze blocks, the staircase is cast concrete, and the floor is a mix of resin and sand

for accessibility. As well as being served by a lift big enough for a wheelchair, there are wide doorways, level thresholds and an extra-large bathroom, plus fittings have been installed to allow the future addition of handrails. 'It's a senior home, but it doesn't look like a senior home yet,' says van Oppen. 'You don't want all the brackets installed when you're only 60.'

Other configurations offer solutions for when the children grow beyond adolescence and start seeking independence. On the first and second floors, rooms on the north side of the building could be split off to create either one or two compact studio flats, so young adults could have their own space without having to move out.

With these different options planned from the outset, it was possible to design electrical and service systems to be easily divided – although in the end, van Oppen only did it for one other configuration. 'Being in one family, it's not going to be a major issue,' he says, 'but it would have been more elegant to be able to separate completely.'

One challenge to designing a house in this way is that everyone needs to be in agreement when it comes to material finishes, otherwise spaces become disjointed. Luckily for van Oppen, his family didn't mind his choice of industrial materials, which include breeze-block walls, steel balustrades, cast concrete staircases, and a floor made from a mix of epoxy resin and quartz sand. Together they create an interior that is highly practical. The resin floor, for instance, means the bathroom and shower areas can be simply wiped clean.

Creative furniture solutions

Bespoke furniture elements also support the building's flexibility. In the second-floor master bedroom, instead of fixed partition walls, full-height cabinets made from oriented strand board (OSB) divide the sleeping area from the en-suite bathroom and dressing room.

Similarly, the master bedroom for the upper apartment is framed by mahogany cabinets that integrate sliding doors, so the space can be closed off or made to feel more open-plan. Even the pot plants are on castors, so they can be moved around the building without fuss.

3 Generation House offers ingenious solutions to the challenges that face every modern family. It shows how multigenerational living can become a long-term lifestyle choice, not just a temporary fix. The project has proved so successful that van Oppen is now working with a property developer to scale the idea up for mass housing. 'I think many people can benefit from housing that is a bit more integrated,' adds the architect. 'Friends of mine were sceptical, but I would recommend it to anyone. You're travelling less, you have more free time and there's more care for each other. I only see benefits.'

Fig 4.1.5 Mahogany cabinets integrate sliding doors, allowing a bedroom space to be opened up or closed off

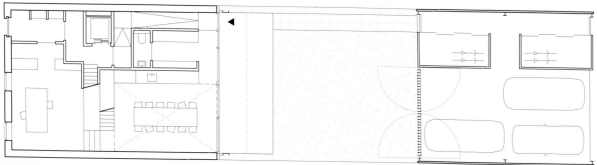

Fig 4.1.6a Ground floor plan

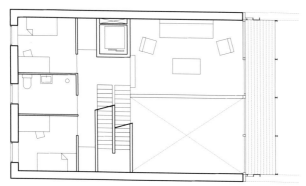

Fig 4.1.6b First floor plan

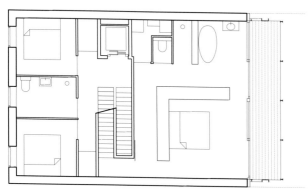

Fig 4.1.6c Second floor plan

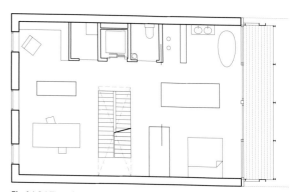

Fig 4.1.6d Third floor plan

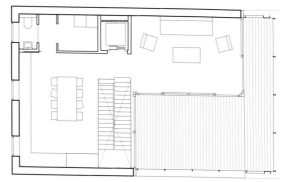

Fig 4.1.6e Fourth floor plan

Case study: Caring Wood

Client: Confidential

Architect: James Macdonald Wright, Niall Maxwell

Type: Private residence

Location: Kent, UK

Completion year: 2017

Gross internal floor area: 1,443sqm

This reinvention of the traditional English country house was named RIBA House of the Year in 2017, precisely because it offers a new model for multifamily living. What at first glance looks like a grandiose villa is in fact a combined home for four factions of an extended family. At each of its corners is a self-contained residence, designed in the spirit of the oast houses that feature throughout the surrounding Kent landscape, while the central section contains a variety of shared spaces, including a cosy communal kitchen, a contemplative courtyard, and a gallery for hosting art exhibitions and music recitals. It offers its residents a wealth of opportunities to spend time together and support one another, but also the ability to easily retreat back into solitude when desired or needed.

Layers of privacy

The architects behind Caring Wood are James Macdonald Wright, a member of the client family, and friend Niall Maxwell, founder of the studio Rural Office for Architecture. The driving force was Macdonald Wright's father-in-law, who for some time had been thinking about how he and his wife could live more closely to their three daughters, along with various

Fig 4.2.1 Resembling Kent's traditional oast houses, Caring Wood was designed to house four factions of an extended family

Fig 4.2.2 and 4.2.3 There is only one kitchen, encouraging residents to cook and eat all together. The scale is cosy and domestic, despite the size

partners and children. Inspired by many vacations spent together inside large rental properties, they came up with an idea for a grouping of distinct but connected homes. It is by no means a low-budget house, yet the extravagance of some of its amenities – like a dedicated snooker room and a home cinema – is lessened by the fact that they are shared between the equivalent of four households. At the same time, the design explores how collective living can truly bring a family together.

'You have to think about layers of privacy,' explains Macdonald Wright. 'In a larger-scale house like this, not everyone is as close to each other as they are to their direct family, so you have to think about how that is going to work.' While a typical home might include two layers, namely the private bedrooms and the communal family living spaces, Caring Wood has four. As well as bedrooms and en-suites, each of the four family units has its own lounge and bathroom, along with spaces specific to the occupants, like study areas or guest rooms. But the shared spaces at the centre of the house also come in two varieties: at a domestic level are rooms for cooking, dining and relaxing, while the gallery was envisioned as a setting for public events and social gatherings.

Changing scales

Externally Caring Wood reads as five buildings, set at different levels on the hillside. They are all demarcated by tall, clay-tile roofs, much like the pointed roofs of traditional oast houses, which were designed for the purpose of drying hops. But inside, the junctions between different types of space are more subtle and varied. There are doors marking the entrance

Fig 4.2.4 and 4.2.5 Grand spaces at the heart of the home include a gallery, designed to host musical recitals and art exhibitions, and a contemplative courtyard

Fig 4.2.6 Simple bedrooms and bathrooms feature throughout, so as not to create tensions between different family members, young and old

to each corner house, but other areas are separated simply by changes in level. There are also visible differences in ceiling heights and in the widths of corridors and staircases. Broadly, the more people that are likely to use a space, the grander it is in scale. However, that doesn't mean that all of the communal rooms are huge; in fact the kitchen and dining room are proportionally quite small, making them just as comfortable for four or five people as they would be for the whole extended family.

A lot of thought went into these rooms in particular, explains Macdonald Wright. It was a conscious decision from the outset to have just one kitchen in the entire building; as the family had always taken pleasure in cooking and eating together, it made sense to encourage this. 'It became like a village square, a hub of the house,' says the architect. 'People just enjoy hanging out in the kitchen when others are there.'

Good relations between residents were ensured by giving everyone (grandparents and grandchildren alike) equally simple bedroom and bathroom facilities. There is no hierarchy when it comes to age or position in the family, and thus no fuel for underlying tensions.

Greater freedoms

You might think that life at Caring Wood would be hectic, with the constant comings and goings of its many residents, but what Macdonald Wright and his family realised soon after moving in was that the house afforded them a level of freedom they had not experienced before. With so many adults around,

someone can nip out to the shops without telling anyone, while a small group can go to the pub at a moment's notice without having to find a babysitter. Equally, group activities can take place in a home of this scale without needing to involve everyone. 'When you put that many people into one house, it allows you a degree of selfishness,' explains the architect. 'If somebody wants to play Scrabble, but that's the last thing you want to do, it doesn't matter. Three or four people will be playing before you know it, and you can go and do something else.'

Another thing that became apparent was that, while adults need the layers of privacy that this home provides, to children these boundaries are meaningless. For the seven children of this family, the whole house became a playground. 'The children would say, we want to sleep in that room because it's near the table tennis, or we want to stay with our cousins to read a book together,' says Macdonald Wright. In this way, the building's design nurtures social skills that can be lacking in children from small family households, but that likely prove fruitful as they develop personal and professional relationships in later life.

Caring Wood is a brave exploration into how multiple families, across different generations, can offer one another emotional, physical and financial support, without sacrificing their independence. As social structures evolve, and people become increasingly isolated by digital devices, this house shows how collectives (familial or otherwise) can benefit from and enjoy togetherness.

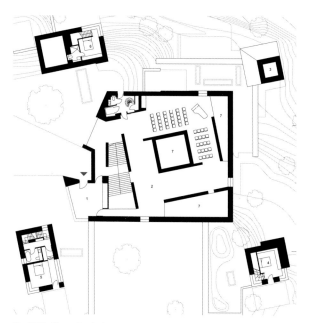

Fig 4.2.7a Upper level plan

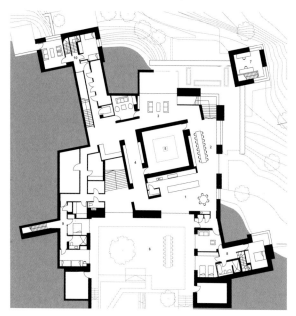

Fig 4.2.7b Mid-level plan

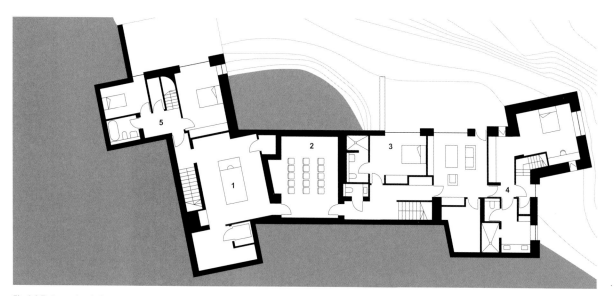

Fig 4.2.7c Lower level plan

Case study: Angel Gardens

Operator: Moda Living

Architects: Haus, Ryder

Interior designer: Naomi Cleaver

Type: Build-to-rent

Location: Manchester, UK

Completion year: 2020

Gross internal floor area: 51,534sqm

Angel Gardens represents a new generation of apartment buildings that are purpose-built for rent, containing both family-size homes and shared amenity spaces. In the US, where the concept is well established, the model is known colloquially as multifamily, while in the UK we call it build-to-rent (BTR).

This is not called co-living, because unlike the schemes that come under this category (where private apartments are typically small studios), the apartments in a BTR scheme like Angel Gardens are of a standard, if not expansive size. Yet in many ways, BTR is just a different form of shared living, offering a rental model that allows couples and families to live closer together, not just singles.

The demand is clearly there. Over the last 10 years, the number of households in the private rented sector has grown by 63%, while the percentage of owner-occupiers has declined, and this trend is set to continue.[4] There are a number of reasons for this, from obstacles to home ownership to the perception that borrowing to buy a home is a burden. Whatever the reasons, BTR offers an attractive alternative. It brings much-needed quality and innovation to the private rented sector, as well as volume in the face of substantial housing undersupply across all sectors – according to research commissioned by the National Housing Federation and Crisis, an additional 340,000 homes need to be built each year in order to meet demand.[5]

A broader audience

Angel Gardens is one of the first BTR projects in the UK, containing 466 apartments, with interiors by Naomi Cleaver. It offers a mix of studios, one- and two-bedroom flats, and three-bedroom penthouses, all available for rent. Here, the shared aspects that make the co-living model so innovative are combined with spacious, comfortable living spaces with mass appeal. This is renting reinvented, with concierge-style services and amenities all part of the package – no more waiting in for the plumber, or going out to find a gym.

Penthouses don't come cheap – at the time of writing, they were being rented at around £6,000 per month – but there are also more affordable options. For instance, there are two-bed sharer apartments that allow two flatmates to cohabit (each with their own large en-suite bedroom) for around £800 per month. Such breadth in appeal has been made possible as a result of Naomi designing all of the apartment furniture, which is unique to the scheme.

Fig 4.3.1 In the reception area, bespoke design details reference the site's history as home to the UK's first steam-powered cotton mill

Angel Gardens occupies the site of Shudehill Mill, the UK's first steam-powered cotton mill, so motifs that celebrate Manchester's historic textile industry, of raw materials and the theatre of production, were used. These work in parallel with the drama of the building itself, one of Manchester's tallest tower blocks.

The rounded shape of the reception desk was designed to emulate the cogs in a spinning machine, while a lighting feature high above consists of cables that wrap around steel members like skeins of cotton. Texture is privileged over colour to create a sensual, homely atmosphere with instinctive appeal, but also to attenuate sound in a large, glassy volume; parquet limestone forms the flooring and a feature wall made from folds of cotton fabric frames a fireplace.

Sharing can be fun

Amenities include an 'insta-sensation' branded gym and a fitness studio with a programme of free-access exercise classes. In the seventh floor communal suite, there is also a screening room with voluptuous coral velvet seating and a large kitchen/dining room. Along with a custom-made kitchen in blue steel, it features a dining table with a top that announces in brass letters, 'A TABLE IS FOR DANCING ON', to quote Manchester impresario, Tony Wilson.

A spacious adjacent lounge is subdivided through furniture groupings, signalling different propositions, from sitting around the fire reading the papers, to working at a laptop with a freshly squeezed juice at the bar, watching the game on squishy denim-

upholstered sofas or just watching the rain, for which Manchester is infamous, through full-height windows with views to the Lancashire Peak District beyond. Outside, the party continues: on the roof terrace is a sports pitch with a full chef's kitchen and barbecue.

But it is the design of the back-of-house which makes this scheme work. Service is front and centre of the best BTR propositions, and motivated staff equals satisfied residents who will want to maintain their

tenancy; management offices at Angel Gardens have been considered with just the same attention to detail as private apartments, and generous storage can stow parcels, groceries and dry-cleaning for residents until they collect.

In a city that's home to two Premier League football teams (each with a large and transient staff) and is a major commercial centre, premium rental accommodation like this, which feels like a favourite hotel, is a welcome addition.

Fig 4.3.4 In addition to the main lounge, there are a number of other spaces where residents can relax, including a library where bookshelves span floor to ceiling

Fig 4.3.5 A cinema room is furnished with reclining seating in coral velvet

Fig 4.3.6 There are several co-working spaces dotted throughout the building, along with bookable meeting rooms, making it easy to work from home

Fig 4.3.7 From one-bedroom studios to three-bedroom penthouses, apartments are designed to feel spacious and luxurious, allowing residents to find privacy when they need it

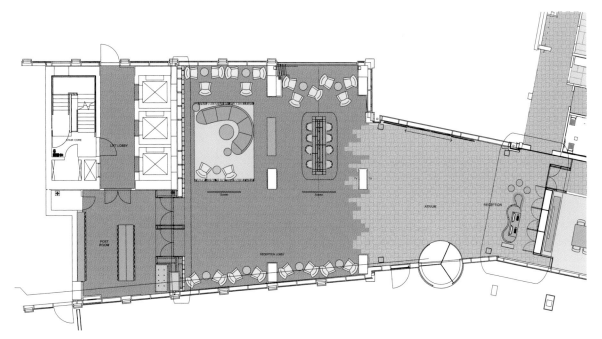

Fig 4.3.8 Ground floor plan

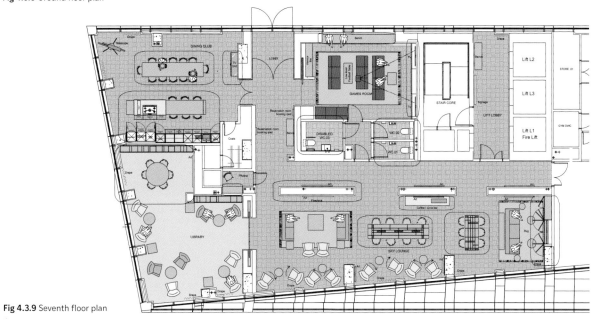

Fig 4.3.9 Seventh floor plan

Case study: Lange Eng

Operator/Client: Lange Eng Cohousing Community

Architect: Dorte Mandrup Arkitekter

Landscape architect: Marianne Levinsen Landskab

Type: Owner-occupied co-housing

Location: Albertslund, Denmark

Completion year: 2009

Gross internal floor area: 6,400sqm

Lange Eng explores a middle ground between Denmark's radical mid-century co-housing communities and the suburban family homes of the 21st century. For its residents, who organised and funded the entire project themselves, it recreates the community spirit of the 1960s model, but without compromising the freedoms that come with owning your own home. It shows that sharing doesn't have to mean sacrifice.

Located on the outskirts of Copenhagen, the complex consists of 54 owner-occupied homes that are much like those of any new residential development. Designed by Danish firm Dorte Mandrup Arkitekter, the properties are compact but not meagre in size, each with separate entrances, living rooms, kitchens and bathrooms. At the same time, there are facilities that encourage all 200 residents to spend time together. Instead of private gardens, each home opens on to one large communal courtyard, while a common house allows everyone to share their meals. 'It's co-living without that imposed commune feel,' explains Kasper Pilemand, associate partner and senior architect at Dorte Mandrup Arkitekter. 'You can choose to be communal here, but you don't have to.'

Community not commune

The project was initiated by a group of six young families, who had outgrown their homes in Copenhagen but weren't ready to give up the social aspect of city life. They realised that joining forces would give them more options, so they formed a co-housing cooperative and invited others to join them. Unlike the co-housing communities of the 1960s and 1970s, pioneered by architect Jan Gudmand-Høyer and activist Bodil Graae, the goal here was not to invent a new lifestyle. They weren't looking for an alternative to the nuclear family, but to simply exploit the practical advantages of shared living. Some of the group had themselves been raised in these co-housing projects, so were especially cautious about creating homes that would compromise their privacy. 'There was strong opposition to the imposed community, particularly from those with experience of the communes,' says Pilemand. 'At the same time, there was a strong ideology. They didn't want to live in single units; they wanted to strengthen their community.'

'Semi-private zones' are one of the features that allow Lange Eng to strike a functional balance between public and private. These are spaces that would traditionally be private, but which offer greater benefits to residents because they are open. For instance, every home has two entrances – one that leads in from the street and a second that connects with the courtyard – but both are designed to encourage neighbourly interactions.

On the outside, steel staircases offer the same feeling of enclosure and security as a hedge or fence might, but also create spaces where people feel inclined to hang

Fig 4.4.1 Lange Eng's 54 homes share a large communal courtyard, instead of individual gardens, making it easier for children to play with others

Fig 4.4.2 and 4.4.3 Staircases create semi-private spaces at the entrance to each home, while contrasting materials differentiate between external and courtyard facades

out, whether on the steps or underneath. In the same spirit, the courtyard entrances are outlined by a single, continuous deck. It is shared by all, yet everyone has their own portion to claim. They do this with barbecues and patio furniture, extending their living rooms out into the collective domain.

Making life easier

This balance between private and public extends to many other aspects of life at Lange Eng. In the Common House, each household is obligated to cook for its neighbours at least once in every cycle, using groceries they source themselves. In return, they have dinner provided for them six days a week. Canteen-style tables and benches create a welcoming, communal dining room, but residents can choose to pick up takeaway meals to enjoy in their homes. The idea is to make life easier, not just more sociable.

Other communal facilities are designed with practicality in mind. The common house includes robust, multipurpose rooms for yoga classes, craft workshops or children's parties. There is no common launderette, as all homes have their own washing machines, but there is a shared workshop and 'garden shed'. Even the garden is designed to be usable in all seasons, not just during the short Danish summer. Designed by landscape architect Marianne Levinsen, it marries intimate spaces with generous play areas and a common thoroughfare. 'With an enclosed courtyard, you have the ability to oversee the space,' says Pilemand, 'but it's also big enough for you to go out and hide when you want to.' The community is just as present digitally as it is physically. Through the Forum web portal, residents can organise babysitting, join sports clubs or air their grievances, while a car club serves those without their own transport.

Fig 4.4.4 Meals are served six days a week in the common house, but residents can choose whether to eat in or take away

Fig 4.4.5 Homes are much like any other, with their own kitchens, bathrooms and living spaces, to give residents as much flexibility as possible

Soft boundaries

Material choices help to both lessen and reinforce boundaries in different ways. The outer facade is clad in black-painted timber, a material that is welcoming, but still presents a barrier to intruders. By contrast, the courtyard-facing walls are translucent polycarbonate, softening the border between inside and out as much as possible. 'Instead of having to walk through a massive house, you actually walk through a membrane,' says Pilemand. A downside to this strategy is that it discourages relationships between Lange Eng and other Albertslund communities – something the project has been criticised for.[6] But some walls are needed, Pilemand argues, as without them it's difficult to establish any sense of belonging. 'It's not about making a castle,' he says. 'It's about making a wall to the world, but then inviting the world to enter.'

In the 10 years since Lange Eng was completed, residents have come and gone, and rules have changed, but the community spirit endures. Its architecture provides a framework for new lifestyles, even those that are still being established, and proves that suburban life doesn't have to mean isolation. As long-term resident Laura Juvik explains: 'Our homes are a big circle holding hands.'

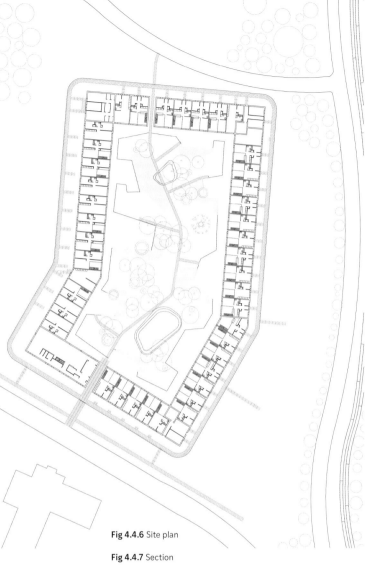

Fig 4.4.6 Site plan

Fig 4.4.7 Section

Case study: New Ground Cohousing

Operator/Client: Older Women's Cohousing

Architect: Pollard Thomas Edwards

Type: Owner-occupied and socially rented senior co-housing

Location: London, UK

Completion year: 2016

Gross internal floor area: 2,394sqm

As the UK's first senior co-housing community, New Ground is home to Older Women's Cohousing (OWCH), a group of 26 women all over the age of 50. Inspired by examples in the Netherlands, Switzerland and Denmark, this residential complex in north London is a pioneering model for how older people can live with dignity in their later years, supporting one another rather than relying on outside help. Residents have full autonomy over their lives, are part of an active community and have homes they feel proud of. In many ways New Ground is like the co-living developments aimed at younger people, with opportunities for both privacy and sociability, but there is one crucial difference; this is not a place where people are coming and going as they move between jobs and cities, it is a home where residents plan to spend the rest of their lives. That sense of commitment is reflected in every aspect of the development.

The complex consists of 25 flats, with 17 owner-occupied and eight socially rented by charity Housing for Women. These are contained in a pair of two- and three-storey brick buildings, which take their design cues from a group of neighbouring cottages built in the 19th century.

Homes are arranged around a large shared garden, with balconies and terraces facing towards it. There's also a common house where the community can come together for meals and social activities, an apartment for guests to stay and a communal launderette.

Taking an active role in retirement

OWCH is responsible for everything. Not only does the group handle the management and upkeep of the complex, it was instrumental in both its inception and its construction. It all started when founding members Madeleine Levius and Shirley Meredeen attended a workshop led by co-housing expert Maria Brenton, who was presenting research into how shared living can offer greater independence and sociability in retirement. Buoyed by the idea of being able to live out their final years without moving to a care home or imposing on family, the duo recruited more like-minded women to join them. With Brenton's help, they formed a partnership with non-profit housing association Hanover, which found them a site in High Barnet and connected them with architects' office Pollard Thomas Edwards.

Pollard Thomas Edwards was already an advocate for giving older people more control over their housing, having argued for it in *HAPPI*, a national report into senior housing co-authored by the firm.[7] In keeping with that ethos, the practice let OWCH lead the design process. 'They had a really well-developed way of making decisions,' explains Patrick Devlin, partner at Pollard Thomas Edwards, and the architect who led the project. 'They had spent a lot of time discussing their

Fig 4.5.1 New Ground consists of 25 flats, each with their own terraces and balconies, organised around a large garden that residents maintain themselves

Fig 4.5.2 and 4.5.3 A common house hosts occasional shared meals and social activities. The rule is that residents are welcome to attend any event held there, to make it as inclusive as possible

ethos and their priorities, but they didn't have any fixed conception of what a development for the rest of their lives should look like'.

The design developed over several months; through a series of workshops, they collaboratively worked out every functional detail, from the form of the buildings through to flat layouts and entrance locations. After planning permission was granted and every OWCH member had been assigned a flat, Pollard Thomas Edwards also hosted 'design surgeries' where residents could rework the internal layouts of their homes to suit their specific lifestyles and preferences. It was a lengthy process but an essential one, says Devlin. 'It takes a long time to absorb these kinds of quantities of information when you're coming to something entirely new,' he explains.

Homes that promote wellbeing

The homes are designed to be practical, comfortable and accessible in equal measure, whether the occupant is 50 years old or 90. While they adhere to most recognised space standards for wheelchair accessibility, they don't follow the rules blindly. So while every home has a level threshold and a large bathroom, the kitchens are more compact, to keep them feeling domestic rather than institutional. 'There is no excuse and no medical reason for making a flat look like a care home; it's inhuman,' says Devlin. 'It's important to realise that other things are more important to people's mental health and wellbeing.' Natural light and ventilation were high on the list of priorities. Every home has dual-aspect windows and a private balcony or terrace, and those on the upper storeys also feature lofty ceilings.

Fig 4.5.4 and 4.5.5 Homes are designed to feel domestic rather than institutional. All are largely wheelchair accessible, and equal priority was given to qualities like natural daylight and ventilation

The common house hosts a range of activities like drawing classes and yoga sessions, as well as more casual socialising. It sits in a central location, at the point where the two housing blocks intersect, yet it doesn't serve as an entrance. Every home has its own front door, so residents are free to come and go without any pressure to stop and chat, but they all pass by the common house on their way in and out, making it easy to pop in when they feel like it. It is a way for the building to encourage social relationships without imposing them, particularly when the garden already functions as a community hub.

A self-sufficient community

The same thinking applies to the way spaces and processes are managed. OWCH members are expected to participate in the running of the building, but this is organised on a volunteer basis. One group takes care of the finances, for instance, while another manages legal issues. There's a group that maintains the garden and another that runs the communal kitchen, preparing shared meals one day a week. Budget can be allocated to outsource certain tasks when it makes sense – mowing the lawn being a prime example – but the group is otherwise unreliant on outside help. Unlike a care home, they place very little strain on local services. Even if a resident falls sick, their neighbours are usually there to cover responsibilities and even deliver meals.

New Ground challenges the assumptions that shared living is for young people and that senior housing is only for the needy. In the UK, over three million people over the age of 70 live alone, and two-thirds of these are women, thanks to longer life expectancies and imbalances in the age profiles of married couples.[8] At the same time, loneliness is a proven cause of mental health issues, dementia and premature death.[9] But here, 26 women of different ages, races and backgrounds are proving there is an alternative. Many describe it as the best home they've ever had. 'One of the keys to remaining happy and healthy as you get older is having a home that reflects your personality,' adds Devlin. 'The more domestic it can be, and flexible to your needs, the happier you're going to be there.'

Social space
One bedroom apartment
Two bedroom apartment
Three bedroom apartment
Ancillary space

Fig 4.5.6a Ground floor plan

Fig 4.5.6b First floor plan

Social space
One bedroom apartment
Two bedroom apartment
Three bedroom apartment
Ancillary space

Fig 4.5.6c Second floor plan

Case study: Humanitas Deventer

Operator: Humanitas Deventer

Type: Nursing home with student accommodation

Location: Deventer, the Netherlands

Completion year: 2012 ongoing

This elderly care home in the Netherlands demonstrates how it's possible to bring the very old together with the very young. Humanitas Deventer houses 150 senior citizens, but it also offers free accommodation to six university students. Instead of rent, these twentysomethings are asked to spend 30 hours a month with their elderly neighbours. There's no care work involved; they simply hang out together, sharing meals, taking walks and playing games. This has a visible impact on the happiness and healthiness of the older residents, but younger residents also feel the benefits. As well as making student living more affordable, it allows these young adults to learn about the life experiences of a completely different generation and understand the value of slowing down.

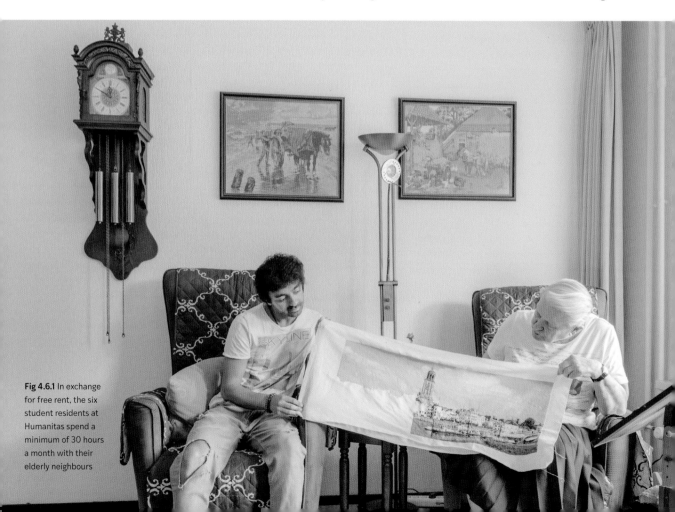

Fig 4.6.1 In exchange for free rent, the six student residents at Humanitas spend a minimum of 30 hours a month with their elderly neighbours

Humanitas was not designed in the traditional sense. Unlike the other case studies in this book, its innovative nature has come about through changes in operation, rather than architecture. When the facility was first built in 1965, it was no different from any other nursing home. It wasn't until 2012, when Gea Sijpkes joined as managing director, that changes were put in place. Sijpkes believes firmly that an end-of-life home should share the same warmth and conviviality as any other home rather than feel institutionalised, or it will start to breed feelings of isolation, dependence and depression. Mental wellbeing is just as important as physical wellbeing, she explains, so while medical care must of course play a role, it can't define the space alone. Even in very old age, there has to be more to life than being fed, watered and looked after. 'Life cannot be reduced to a simple need for care,' Sijpkes says. 'The focus needs to be on maintaining wellbeing and emphasising life.'

Fig 4.6.2 Spaces are designed to feel homely rather than institutional. Examples include a lounge space that doubles as a community library

A live-in experiment

Intergenerational living was the first big experiment Sijpkes was able to introduce. Although the board were shocked when she first proposed the idea, convinced that the 'sex, drugs and rock 'n' roll culture' of young people would be dangerous for 'fragile' residents, they initially agreed to test the concept by allowing a single student to move in. Sijpkes was insistent that there should be no rules – she wanted to shake things up. So the arrival of party-loving Onno Selbach proved challenging at first, as staff got used to him coming and going in the early hours. But the atmosphere soon changed for the better, as residents started taking more of an interest in 'their student' and stopped asking about doctors' appointments and absent relatives. Selbach changed too, becoming more patient and empathetic than before.

Fig 4.6.3 The interior design includes bright colours, patterned wallpaper and large-scale photos, while essential oils are used to create welcoming smells

Fig 4.6.4 The building includes a gym that is open to the community. Walls are painted with the colours and badge of the local football team

Things continued to improve as more young people were invited in. Students started playing drinking games with the seniors and challenging them to wheelchair races in the hallways. They taught them how to use social media and challenged them on their views about topics like premarital sex.[10] The home became a place where everyone, no matter their age, could find something to smile about.

Bringing outsiders in

With the success of the student living programme, Sijpkes was able to introduce more initiatives that allow the residents of Humanitas to interact with the neighbourhood. With a goal of creating 'the warmest house in the neighbourhood', the building began hosting an array of community clubs and events, from support groups to sewing clubs. Key to this approach was making the building appear welcoming, so it felt more like a home than a hospital. Spaces achieve this by appealing to all of the senses. Essential oils and natural ventilation make rooms feel fresh and fragrant. Walls are covered in bright colours, wallpaper and photos, to 'lift spirits and lighten moods'. There's a tea and coffee station that serves free drinks to everyone in the community, and an aviary where residents and guests can enjoy listening to birdsong.

'There is plenty of evidence that shows that the physical environment can have a major impact on people's overall feeling of wellbeing,' says Sijpkes. 'We explored small, quick-win solutions to make the home a more pleasant place for our residents.'

The spaces of Humanitas are styled with a sense of fun, familiarity and humour. There's a room made to look like a traditional Dutch 'brown bar' with timber-lined walls, chunky wooden furniture and a dartboard. There's a lounge that doubles as a community library, lending books to anyone that wants to borrow them. In the gym, which is open to visitors as well as residents, walls are painted with the colours and badge of the local football team, while the basement has been transformed into a 'train club' by a group of local autistic children with a love of model trains. 'We started with the interior and moved on, with our core values to guide us, to create an inclusive community,' explains Sijpkes.

A model for change

Humanitas has come to describe itself as a 'living lab', where social experiments are used to forge greater connections between people. Because community spirit drove the design, rather than the other way around, its spaces respond directly to the needs of the neighbourhood both inside and outside the building. These experiments have had tangible results, not just socially but financially. As well as its students, Humanitas now provides accommodation and support for young people with mild mental disabilities, saving the state thousands of euros every year. Yet the facility still manages to maintain a net profit margin of at least 5% per year, which is better than the national average.[11] The building is living proof that a more inclusive approach to the design of care spaces makes sense in every way.

Fig 4.7.1 At Serenbe, homes are built close together to make them more space-efficient, but also to create more opportunities for interaction between neighbours

Case study: Serenbe

Client: Steve and Marie Nygren

Architect: Serenbe Planning & Design

Urban planner: Phillip Tabb

Type: Newbuild agrihood

Location: Chattahoochee Hills, Georgia, United States

Completion year: 2004 ongoing

Gross area: 4.4km²

'People that move here are people that are filled with hope, because they see that there's a better tomorrow,' says Steve Nygren, describing the new neighbourhood he has been building on the outskirts of Atlanta, Georgia. Called Serenbe, a reworking of the phrase 'be serene', it is a place that has very little in common with today's towns and cities, in that it boasts a strong sense of community, and prioritises health and wellbeing above all else. Here, people wave to you when you pass them on the street, the food you eat comes from the local land, and it's not unusual for people to hike several miles every day.

Serenbe is what's known as an agrihood, a community structured around nature and agriculture. It's based on biophilic principles – the idea that people live happier and healthier lives when they are more connected to the natural world. So at Serenbe, a farm is the heart of the neighbourhood, and idyllic countryside (complete with 15 miles of trails) provides the surroundings. But nature's not the only thing that sets this place apart; its buildings and spaces are designed to encourage social interactions, amenities are there to be shared,

Fig 4.7.2 and 4.7.3 Houses come in various architectural styles, both modern and traditional, but an essential feature is a large front porch or veranda, so each home can open up to the neighbourhood

and people of different ages live together. It is a development underpinned by many of the same principles driving the co-living movement, albeit on a much larger scale.

Bringing density to the countryside

Nygren's project was originally about preservation in the face of urban sprawl. Having swapped city life in Atlanta for a quiet retreat in the countryside, he and his wife Marie were alarmed to one day discover bulldozers razing land nearby. To fend off the suburbanisation he feared was on its way, Nygren decided to develop the land himself, with a different approach. Inspired by traditional English villages, his vision was for a small settlement with relative density, so that only 30% of the rural land would become urbanised and the rest would be protected as a nature reserve.

Since the first house was completed in 2004, Serenbe has grown to include a series of 'hamlets', containing more than 350 homes. It's similar to co-housing, in that people own or rent entire houses (rather than sharing any of their main living spaces), and the community spirit is generated in the areas that surround them. These houses come in a diverse mix of architectural styles – a deliberate move, says Nygren, to create natural variety – but they all follow a series of urban planning guidelines drawn up by town planner and placemaking expert Phillip Tabb. This ensures that properties are not only space-efficient, but that they avoid the issues of social isolation that typically arise in suburban neighbourhoods.

Fig 4.7.4 A community farm is the heart of the neighbourhood. Residents can opt into a scheme where they take home a share of the harvest, but there's also a farmers' market every weekend

Fig 4.7.5 Community spaces
are dotted throughout the
neighbourhood. Local shops
often include seating areas, while
post is delivered to centralised
'mail stations'

First, homes are all built close together, with large porches that extend out to the pavement. In certain locations, the requirement is for these verandas to be at least 2m wide, to ensure frequent conversations between neighbours and passersby. 'Most people are very comfortable going on their neighbours' front porches and chatting, which is especially great for the older people,' says Nygren. 'Some have health issues that mean they can't get out, but they can sit on their front porch and people feel free to come and have a five-minute conversation with them, without having to take the time for a full visit.'

Second, functional community spaces are dotted through each of the hamlets. Post is delivered to local 'mail stations' rather than to individual homes, and these are mostly positioned alongside playgrounds and cafes. 'A common joke at Serenbe is it takes two hours to get your mail,' reveals Nygren. In the same spirit, many local stores and restaurants incorporate some element of casual hospitality, where you could pull up a chair to work on a laptop, or grab a coffee with friends.

There's also a 'country inn' containing 27 guest rooms, so locals don't need to own a big house to be able to invite friends and family to stay.

The ambition throughout is to create places where people feel comfortable and welcome. 'With this inclusive type of land plan, neighbours know neighbours in a very significant way, unlike in places they have lived before,' says Nygren. 'Of course we have some households where one spouse is on the front porch and knows everyone on the street, and the other spouse takes the back door. But on average, people report that they're at least twice as engaged here as wherever they were living before.'

Room for variety

With such an active community, there's a wide range of local groups and regular events taking place, and Serenbe's various hamlets are structured to facilitate these. Art is the focus in Selborne, with initiatives in place to support local creative talent, while Mado places emphasis on wellbeing, with gardens full of medicinal plants and activities like goat yoga. The Grange hamlet centres around the farm, with volunteer days and educational workshops so that everyone can get involved. Many of the residents opt in to a community supported agriculture (CSA) scheme, where they take home a share of the harvest every week, and there's a farmers' market every weekend.

Landscaping is used to reinforce these messages. Instead of fences, fruit trees and bushes line the streets so that residents can always find themselves a healthy snack, while rubbish bins are stored underground to keep the landscape looking clean.

Nygren believes that Serenbe residents all have two things in common: a passport and a sense of optimism. That is to say that everyone has a global outlook, which perhaps makes them appreciate the value of slow living more than most, and they have a shared willingness to try new things and change the status quo. However, living in Serenbe is less of a culture shock than you might think. Despite the countryside setting, it is conveniently located less than an hour's drive from Atlanta, which itself is home to one of the world's largest and busiest airports. This means that living in Serenbe doesn't have to mean cutting yourself off from the rest of the world, and there's less pressure for this neighbourhood to be completely self-sufficient in terms of employment and services. In fact, around 30% of Serenbe's residents use this as their vacation home rather than their main residence, making it all the more impressive that it has managed to cultivate such a close-knit community. It's testament to the value system that is embedded in the design, and proves that the concepts of shared living and community building are bound up with the fundamentals of good urban planning.

With construction underway on a fourth hamlet, the Serenbe team are finding even more ways of using architecture to bring residents closer together. Nygren is exploring the possibility of multigenerational homes – his three daughters all live in the neighbourhood with their own families, and they're keen to combine their households. There are also plans to create dorm-style homes where seniors and students can live alongside one another. Serenbe is fast becoming a place with something to offer everyone.

Fig 5.0.0 Summit House,
London, by Note Design Studio
for The Office Group, 2019

5.
Workplace as community

Co-working as a global movement

While co-living is still a fairly radical concept for many, co-working is something we've all become familiar with. The idea is simple. Instead of owning or leasing your own office space, you simply rent a desk in a shared space. You may not even have a fixed desk, but instead pay a membership fee, for which you get regular or semi-regular access to an office or group of offices. In this way, you can combine the freedom of working for yourself with the community spirit offered by a full-time workplace.

The biggest driver of the co-working movement has of course been the global acceleration of freelance culture. While self-employment was highly uncommon in the 1980s and 1990s, advances in technology have made it far easier for people to become entrepreneurs. Today there are more than four million self-employed workers in the UK alone, while the US counts more than 44 million.[1] For the self-employed, co-working spaces offer multiple benefits. There are opportunities for collaboration and companionship, as well as the obvious advantages for meeting clients, sharing resources and flexibility. But freelancers aren't the only ones interested in co-working; increasingly it is attracting companies, particularly startups. Not only do these workspaces allow businesses to remain nimble in a competitive market, they also promote a culture of innovation and openness among employees. It is not surprising then that

Fig 5.0.1 At its peak, WeWork had approximately 280 properties in 32 different countries, allowing it to become the poster child for the co-working movement

Fig 5.0.2 The Office Group has over 50 co-working spaces in the UK and Germany. Summit House, a London space designed by Note Design Studio, uses soft colours and Art Deco details to create a calming environment for work

co-working has been the biggest trend in commercial real estate in the past decade. There were more than 18,000 co-working spaces in operation worldwide in 2018, and that figure is expected to reach 40,000 by 2024.[2]

There have inevitably been some bumps along the road. The impact of COVID-19 made life very difficult for co-working culture. Most spaces closed during lockdown periods, but those that remained open saw their spaces empty. It still remains to be seen whether these spaces will be able to attract the same volume of users in the future as they did before the lockdowns. But perhaps the biggest roadblock for the co-working trend has been the rise and fall of WeWork, the best-known of all the co-working operators. WeWork's model was simple: lease large spaces from landlords, overhaul the interiors and then find multiple tenants to sublet to. By combining this with a vision for a new work culture, complete with barista coffee and beer on tap, the company was able to attract big investment

and pursue rapid expansion. However, when WeWork went from a valuation of $47 billion to being close to bankruptcy in just six weeks, many questioned whether co-working must just be a fad after all. As it turned out though, the problem wasn't the co-working model, but the business behind it. Fundamentally, WeWork positioned itself as a tech company and used that as an excuse to vastly over-inflate its value. The repercussions were inevitable.[3]

Many of WeWork's competitors are proving that the large-scale serviced office model can be highly effective and profitable, even with the challenges posed by COVID-19. We can see evidence of this from IWG, the company behind co-working brands Regus and Spaces, which announced plans to raise and invest an extra £315 million at a time when many of its offices were shut as a result of lockdown.[4] Similarly, both The Office Group and Fora said they expected to take market share away from traditional offices as a result of the pandemic.[5]

Fig 5.0.3 Second Home teamed up with architect duo SelgasCano to create co-working venues in London, Lisbon and Los Angeles. Offering a mix of different space types, their aim is to promote a culture of collaboration among creative businesses

Communities can be curated

One of the biggest lessons of COVID-19 has been the true role of the office. In the past the office has generally been treated as the place where all work should take place. Following the pandemic, many have realised that remote working is much more effective when it comes to carrying out focused tasks, and that the office (as we formerly understood it) is better used as a space for communication and collaboration. This has big implications for co-working; it means these workspaces need to have spaces where workers can find space and solitude when they need it. But even more importantly, both the spaces and operations need to be designed primarily around a community.

Luckily for co-working, many operators already knew this. Alongside the larger and most well-known providers, there are also hundreds of small-scale co-working companies, many of which set themselves up with a specific community in mind from the outset and use design as a tool to reinforce this. Examples include NeueHouse and Fosbury & Sons, both featured in our case studies, and also Second Home, which has spaces in London, Los Angeles and Lisbon. When entrepreneurs Rohan Silva and Sam Aldenton established Second Home, they designed their entire model around facilitating collaboration between creative businesses. Working with Spanish architect duo SelgasCano, they created spaces designed to promote different forms of creativity. There are no open-plan workspaces; instead translucent partitions and plants frame a rich mix of studio spaces, collaboration areas and events spaces. 'In the Internet age it seems to be more important than ever that people get together

Fig 5.0.4 Fosbury & Sons appeals to a design-savvy audience with its co-working spaces in Belgium and the Netherlands, which all occupy historic buildings. For the Boitsfort venue, the company worked with interiors studio Going East to renovate the CBR Building, a Modernist landmark in Brussels

physically and yet the built environment in the city still seems generic office build,' said Silva, following the launch of the brand's west London venue.[6] 'There's rarely any mixing between companies and it's even more unusual between industries,' he said. 'At Second Home we are really obsessed with trying to drive that cross-pollination, because it is such a driver of innovation; it is the needle we are continuously trying to thread.'

Building a community around a specific group or demographic doesn't come without its challenges, as women-focused members' club The Wing, one of our case studies, disovered to its peril. Set up with the goal of empowering women, The Wing came under fire after failing to navigate issues of gender identity and racial discrimination. While its buildings were designed to promote a spirit of openness and equality, more was needed to marry these ambitions with its operations. It's a cautionary tale for any co-working space looking exclusively to one audience. Ethel's Club, a new co-working space and social club in New York designed for people of colour, is among those that will likely have learned a lot from this example. If you're aware of the risks and able to sidestep them, then these kinds of spaces have the opportunity to create workplaces that are uniquely tailored to their members.

Ultimately the key ingredients in any good co-working space are balance and flexibility. Intelligent design and management need to come in equal measure, in order to create an environment where people will choose to spend time, and spaces need to be adaptable to changing circumstances. Get that right, and it should be plain sailing from there.

Case study: NeueHouse Hollywood

Operator/Client: NeueHouse

Architect/Interior designer: Rockwell Group

Type: Co-working and members' club in converted broadcast studios

Location: Los Angeles, USA

Completion year: 2015

Gross internal floor area: 6,500sqm

A broadcasting centre from radio's golden age is the setting for this Los Angeles co-working complex. In the CBS Radio Building and Studio on Sunset Boulevard – the studios where Orson Welles and Jack Benny took to the airwaves, and where artists like the Beach Boys and Janis Joplin made recordings – a new kind of creative energy is being cultivated. Describing itself as a 'private workspace collective', NeueHouse Hollywood is an environment where any creative agency, large or small, can enjoy the adaptive and collaborative nature of co-working. Looking beyond the shared workplace as a space where individual workers come together, it explores whether this typology can generate a new form of collective company culture.

A fluid approach to workspace

The CBS buildings were designed by Swiss-born Modernist William Lescaze in 1938, combining the crisp lines and right angles of the International Style with the more stylish touches of Streamline Moderne: the curved reveals, porthole windows and glass blocks. Renovated by New York-based architecture and interiors studio Rockwell Group, these spaces retain the style and glamour of old, yet they become more versatile. The recording studios and screening rooms are now part of a multilayered tapestry of workspaces, meeting rooms, events spaces and service areas, able to be used in a number of ways. A flexible partition system allows room layouts to be reconfigured, while some spaces take on different identities from daytime to evening. In this way, programmed events and serendipitous conversations become naturally interwoven in people's daily work routines.

'People had become very fluid about where they wanted to work, where they wanted to live and where they wanted to play, and we saw that as open space to create a co-working place that created a specific culture,' explains architect and Rockwell Group founder David Rockwell. 'We were focusing on the social–cultural possibilities of people coming together and how that could be a generator of ideas.'

Rockwell Group also designed the first NeueHouse in New York, which is significantly smaller than Hollywood but offers similarly fluid spaces. The approach in both cases was to treat the workplace as a form of hospitality, with services designed to provide occupants with a more premium experience but also to create natural rhythms in the day. Part of this comes from food and drink elements, like food carts that deliver at certain times or bars that open up in the evening. There are also lighting systems on manual rigs, which can be raised or lowered to create different kinds of atmosphere. 'It's a question of how you create a place that incentivises people to have spontaneous meetings,' says Rockwell. 'These kinds of rituals are what make hospitality hospitable; it's finding that moment to say hello and interrupt the flow of the day without demanding to be seen.'

A degree of ambiguity

Among the most surprising spaces in NeueHouse Hollywood is Studio A, the theatre where the pilot for *I Love Lucy* was filmed. This is still a place for performance and cinema (it is occasionally rented out by production studios), but it also takes on a more domestic character, with the introduction of globe chandeliers, shaggy rugs and removable furniture. Other spaces on the ground floor have a similarly ambiguous character. There's a double-height gallery where two storeys of glass-fronted meeting rooms are clustered around a more informal lounge space. Elsewhere, an open workspace contains both sofas and oak library tables, interspersed with a coffee bar and leather banquettes. Walls divide different areas, but they are punctured by huge rectangular openings that allow activities to spill across. Lighting also creates different moods, with the combination of large sculptural elements and retro-style desk lamps.

The level of exclusivity increases on the upper floors of the six-storey Radio Building. On the intermediate levels are a mix of desk-filled studios and private offices, framed by the partition system that Rockwell Group designed bespoke for NeueHouse. These partitions make it possible for a company to gradually expand their space as their business grows. Made from cork boards and fluted glass, they have a substantive material quality even though they aren't permanent structures. 'There's a difference between flexible and neutral,' Rockwell points outs. The first and second floors feature spacious members-only roof terraces,

Fig 5.1.1 Studio A, where the pilot for *I Love Lucy* was filmed, functions as a casual meeting space when it's not being used for events or productions

Fig 5.1.2 and 5.1.3 The ground floor contains a mix of open work and lounge spaces, including oak library tables, leather banquettes, sofas, Moroccan rugs and custom-designed chandeliers

taking advantage of LA's good weather, while the fifth floor boasts the Paley Penthouse boardroom (named after CBS founder William Paley), where Bauhaus-inspired furniture and herringbone-patterned oak floors offer a more luxury feel.

Respecting heritage

Throughout the building, materials create a sense of quality. Board-formed concrete walls and exposed pipework might have felt overly industrial, but they are softened by touches of white marble, warm oak, polished steel and Moroccan textiles. Colour is applied sparingly, but there are flashes of deep red and burnt orange. It is not an interior designed to shout; rather it offers a level of sophistication that respects its old Hollywood roots. 'We really just took the DNA of the building,' said Rockwell. 'We were really inspired by the architecture, by the scale of the spaces and by the variety of things we could get in.'

NeueHouse offers a range of membership packages to suit its varied audience. Some choose to work there every day, but others simply come in for meetings and events (it's not uncommon to have a NeueHouse membership in addition to an office elsewhere). Rockwell Group has its own LA outpost in the building, so Rockwell often spends time there himself. He describes the pleasure of peppering his day with unexpected moments, from meeting up with a collaborator for a coffee break, to reaching out to other members for advice on a design, or attending a lecture at the end of the day. In the aftermath of the COVID-19 outbreak, the architect predicts the desire for physical connection in the workplace will mean spaces like NeueHouse become more popular

Fig 5.1.4 A screening room evokes the glamour of old Hollywood, with black wainscoting and linen-upholstered seats

Fig 5.1.5 A flexible partition system, made from cork boards and fluted glass, makes it easy for companies to scale their businesses up or down

than ever. More than co-working, it offers a blend of culture, commerce and hospitality. 'People are curious,' says Rockwell, 'and they want to be around other curious people to see what happens.'

Case study: Fosbury & Sons Harmony

Operator/Client: Fosbury & Sons

Architect/Interior designer: Going East

Type: Co-working in renovated office

Location: Antwerp, Belgium

Completion year: 2016

Gross internal floor area: 5,500sqm

'We wanted to create a home where you can do your job,' says Stijn Geeraets, explaining the concept behind the co-working business he co-founded, Fosbury & Sons. Filled with contemporary art and retro furniture, a Fosbury & Sons venue has a grown-up aesthetic, designed to feel more akin to the home than the office. Unlike the playground-style workspaces popularised by the likes of Google and Facebook, there are no gimmicks – no beanbags, no ping-pong tables and certainly no slides. Instead there are candles, plants, rugs and cushions. Spaces are comfortable *and* aspirational, where work and social lives can agreeably exist side by side, and where people from different industries – be they artists or lawyers – can feel equally at ease.

Fig 5.2.1 The cafe space is one several communal areas in the building. Features include floor ceiling windows and large plar

A mature environment

Every Fosbury & Sons has a bespoke design, although the first set a standard for those that followed. Designed by interiors studio Going East, it occupies the first floor and mezzanine of the WATT-tower, a 1950s building in Antwerp that was once the headquarters of Belgium's largest national electricity supplier. Plaster wall coverings and suspended ceilings have all been stripped out, leaving a space with a raw, industrial finish. At the same time, the addition of lavish textiles, huge planting boxes, solid wood furniture and soft lighting make the interior feel homely. 'We wanted to create a mature, professional environment,' says Geeraets. 'It is a business environment, not a kindergarten, so it needs to be mature. But it also needs to please you. If you feel good in an environment, it has a big impact on your wellbeing.'

For Geeraets, who began his career as a product designer, these ideas started to develop early on. Having spent time in offices where coffee was served

Fig 5.2.2 The design takes its cues from the High Line in New York. A mezzanine level offers opportunities to observe activity taking place on the floor below

in plastic cups, and where inviting a friend or family member to visit was out of the question, he started to think about how a changed workplace could improve his quality of life. The vision started to take shape when Geeraets partnered with Maarten Van Gool, whose background was in marketing and events. They realised that the types of spaces that stimulated their imagination were restaurants, hotels and homes, yet the office was where they spent the majority of their time. Together with real-estate investor Serge Hannecart, they reimagined the office as a business platform. Co-working is central to the concept, but the idea goes beyond the idea of the individual, freelance worker. Private offices and shared workspaces are all part of the mix, and they are accompanied by a variety of communal facilities, lounge areas, meeting rooms and event spaces.

Mixing moods

Altogether, the programme is based around four different brain functions required for work. There are spaces for individual work such as sending emails or carrying out admin tasks, where it can be beneficial to have some background noise and activity. Focus work takes place in quieter, isolated spaces, while collaborative work needs spaces where people can group together. Rest spaces are also important, to allow the brain to process information.

Going East's design for Harmony – the name given to the first Antwerp space – brings these functions together in an arrangement inspired by the High Line in New York. The upper level accommodates private

Fig 5.2.3 and 5.2.4 Seating elements include a bleachers-style staircase that doubles as a presentation or performance space, and a sculpture in the form of a giant cushion

Fig 5.2.5 Candles, plants and textiles help to make spaces feel homely, rather than commercial

rooms, but also serves as a viewing deck overlooking the more active spaces on the floor below. 'We didn't want to create a corridor with a lot of doors; the idea was to make a walk-through space where you feel like you're moving through a city,' explains Going East co-founder Michiel Mertens. 'There is not one direction; you have 50 possible routes to get to your office.' Thanks to this layout, some spaces are more open than others and there are a variety of ceiling heights.

Mertens and partner Anaïs Torfs have furnished spaces accordingly. Their bespoke approach, which includes pairing vintage finds with modern classics and standout artworks, means that every space has a unique character that isn't repeated in other Fosbury & Sons locations. As Mertens points out, the professional community in each city is different. While Antwerp is quite a creative city, Brussels is more about business, and spaces are designed to reflect that.

Moving between spaces

Seating has been carefully selected to facilitate different types of use, and to encourage people to regularly move around. 'We wanted to create a lot of opportunities for you to be in a different environment than behind your desk,' says Mertens. Some chairs are only comfortable to sit in for a few hours, or maybe a day, while others are more ergonomic. There are unusual places to sit down, too, including a bleachers-style staircase that doubles as a presentation or performance space, a spacious daybed and a sculpture in the form of a giant cushion, where people sometimes sit with their laptops on their

knees. Lighting is equally varied, with some rooms deliberately darker than others. Bright fluorescents were avoided as much as possible, and table lamps feature throughout.

'One of the questions we asked ourselves often during the design process was, would we have it in our own homes? Whether the discussion was about a lamp, a plant or a table,' says Geeraets. 'If the answer was no, we didn't integrate it.' These domestic touches extend right down to the details; high-quality headphones offer noise-cancellation, while handmade ceramics are dotted across the bookshelves. 'If you want to feel good in an environment, it has to be a human space,' adds Geeraets. 'We didn't want to create a showroom; it had to be like a home.'

This design approach is what sets Fosbury & Sons apart from other co-working operators. Although the company has several venues in Belgium and more opening up in other European cities, it refuses to adopt a 'copy, paste' approach when it comes to interiors. In complete contrast with Harmony, the Alfons site in Brussels has a bright and airy atmosphere, while the Prinsengracht space in Amsterdam boasts a more formal character. Priority is not given to style, but rather to mood – something that Fosbury & Sons describes as 'joie de vivre'. It's about spaces that promote simple pleasures, like being able to have lunch with your family or watch a ballet performance in your workplace after you've closed up your laptop. Fosbury & Sons shows how the co-working office can make life joyful without being all fun and games.

Fig 5.3.1 The children's area at Big and Tiny Silver Lake features an art room, a playhouse and a ball pond. A programme of activities keeps kids engaged throughout the day

Case study: Big and Tiny Silver Lake

Operator/Client: Big and Tiny

Architect/Interior designer: Zooco

Type: Co-working and childcare in converted warehouse

Location: Los Angeles, USA

Completion year: 2019

Gross internal floor area: 467sqm

As the name suggests, Los Angeles-based Big and Tiny offers facilities for both working parents and young children, without either having to compromise. At its largest space, in Silver Lake, noisy playtime and head-down focus work can take place simultaneously. It is not a kindergarten with a cafe on the side, nor is it a co-working space with a token play area. Here, spaces for adults and kids come in equal measure, and there's a programme of activities for young and old. This means that parents can be productive in their work without being separated from their children, and can become members of an active community that places equal importance on work and family.

The business was founded by Spanish entrepreneur and mother Keltse Bilbao, shortly after she and her family moved to LA. Working from home with two infants had proved impossible, yet Bilbao couldn't find play spaces that worked around her schedule, or with facilities for her as well as the children. She also found it hard to meet other mothers with similar interests. With Big and Tiny, her goal was to merge the co-working model with the children's playground, and at the same time build a community of like-minded working parents. Billed as 'playworking studios', Big and Tiny's spaces offer a variety of flexible membership packages to suit a wide range of lifestyles and budgets.

Work and play can coexist

Spanish architecture studio Zooco designed the Silver Lake location, having already worked on the first Big and Tiny in Santa Monica. Like the business model, the design concept for the interiors aims to blur the boundaries between the personal and the professional.

'Childcare and co-working are completely different worlds with totally opposite needs,' says architect Jorge Alonso. 'We thought it would be an issue, but it became a strength. It led us to create a very neutral and versatile design.' A consistent materials palette runs through the building, made up of simple, natural materials like wood, cardboard, felt and cork. This means that spaces remain visually harmonious, even when they are physically separated, and can easily swap functions when the need arises. For instance, the entire space can be booked out for children's birthday parties.

Housed within a 467sqm warehouse, Big and Tiny Silver Lake is more than twice the size of the first venue and contains a more diverse mix of facilities. While Santa Monica's simple floor plan is divided evenly into three zones (work, play and cafe), Silver Lake's layout is far less arbitrary, providing an assortment of workspace types. There are quiet corners that offer freedom from distractions, open spaces that invite conversation, and a lively cafe where it's possible to keep an eye on the children. There are also breakout areas where members can find solitude and relaxation, including a music studio, a meditation room, a lounge space and an exercise room, along with a communal kitchen where it's possible to prepare food, have a coffee break or warm up a bottle for a baby.

Fig 5.3.2 and 5.3.3 Co-working spaces exist alongside breakout areas, including a music studio, a meditation room and an exercise room, so members can take time out from both work and children

Fig 5.3.4 Natural materials like cardboard, cork and felt help to create a neutral aesthetic throughout the interior, with no distinction between spaces for adults and children

Acoustic solutions

Zooco generated this varied layout with a series of 'cubes' dotted around the building. These self-contained rooms help to organise what is otherwise a largely open-plan space, but also create spaces that can be acoustically sealed from their surroundings. 'After Santa Monica, we learned the importance of acoustic isolation,' explains Alonso. 'Children playing make a lot of noise, but co-working spaces need quiet. If the space is too open you have a lot of issues with noise, so everything has to be designed with acoustics in mind.' Zooco's solution is an insulated, modular panel unit, which forms partition walls and also lines some of the exterior walls. Clad in either cork or felt, these panels offer effective sound barriers and buffers. In the workspaces they double up as pinboards during brainstorming sessions, while in the play area they provide the structure for an art room and a ball pond.

Fig 5.3.5 There are a mix of different workspace types, with acoustic barriers between spaces to allow various activities (including play) to take place at the same time

'Our job as architects is to design spaces that support and enhance the communities we live in, which means you have to be able to use them for more than one function,' adds Alonso. 'We have to learn how to live together like one family.'

Lighting and furniture help to reinforce multifunctionality. Thanks to a number of existing windows and skylights, there is plenty of natural daylight in the space and little issue with glare. Suspended linear fixtures offer additional illumination in the open spaces, while low-hanging pendants offer more focused lighting above

tables or seats that might be used for working, as well as in the enclosed cubes. Chairs and tables are lightweight, making them easy to manoeuvre around, and there's a phone booth so that members can take private calls.

Co-working for families

Big and Tiny's model is one likely to appeal to many. Co-working spaces have become a common fixture in every city[7] and they are no longer just for the young, with many people between the ages of 20 and 50 now using them.[8] However that's not the case for women who have kids, who tend to resort to either working from home or giving up work completely.[9] As Bilbao herself found, parenthood can be lonely and overwhelming, with little opportunity for relief. It seems this demographic has more than most to gain from being part of a supportive community. Big and Tiny shows that there is plenty of scope for the co-working typology to diversify and meet its needs. With more imaginative and flexible design models, there's no reason why it shouldn't continue to be an option for individuals when they decide to start a family.

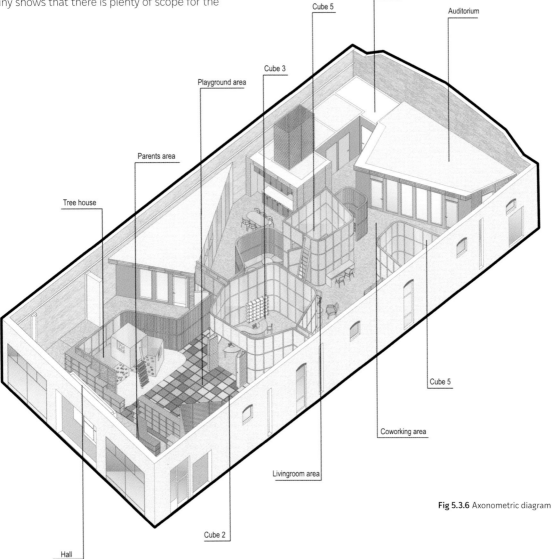

Baños

Cube 5

Auditorium

Cube 3

Playground area

Parents area

Tree house

Cube 5

Coworking area

Livingroom area

Cube 2

Hall

Fig 5.3.6 Axonometric diagram

Case study: The Wing SoHo

Operator/Client: The Wing

Architect: Alda Ly Architecture & Design

Interior designer: Chiara de Rege

Type: Co-working and members' club in converted warehouse

Location: New York, USA

Completion year: 2017–2019

Gross internal floor area: 1,850sqm

The Wing was established to help women thrive in business. With a network of members-only spaces in major US cities, the company set out to offer women a supportive environment in which to work and network. More than just being co-working spaces, the aim behind The Wing's venues was to foster a community of empowered individuals, with amenities and events geared specifically towards a female audience.

The company has faced challenges as a business, following a string of allegations about underlying inequality, specifically towards racial minorities and transgender people, which led to the departure of co-founder Audrey Gelman.[10] Nevertheless, The Wing has pioneered a new workplace aesthetic, offering an alternative to the masculinity of Wall Street. Design was crucial in reinforcing the message; spaces were made to feel feminine without resorting to gender stereotypes. They promoted a message of inclusivity, even if the company wasn't able to match it.

Fig 5.4.1 Common features at The Wing's venues include pastel-coloured furniture, arched doorways and bookshelves organised by colour

Fig 5.4.2 The beauty room, a space filled with hair and makeup products, features bespoke wallpaper that celebrates famous women in New York's history

Helping women to succeed

The business was born out of Gelman's own experiences of working in public relations in New York. Tired of changing outfits in public toilets and charging her phone in hotel lobbies, she envisioned a space that could help women like her navigate a busy schedule, as a place to freshen up and make calls between appointments. After teaming up with business partner Lauren Kassan, Gelman's concept evolved into a space where women could also meet one another and find new opportunities, in the spirit of the women's clubs of the late 19th and early 20th centuries. 'There's something subtly radical about the idea of women taking up space,' Gelman told the *New York Observer* in 2016, following the launch of the inaugural venue in New York's Flatiron district.[11] The aim, she said, was to give women the infrastructure they needed to succeed. 'I hope it serves as a space that satisfies both the need for convenience in women's lives and connection between women who wouldn't normally meet, but find they have much in common.'

The Wing's mix of facilities is unlike that of other co-working spaces or members' clubs. As well as workspaces and lounge areas, every location also features a beauty room filled with styling products, a library containing only books by female or feminist authors, and a 'pump room' where nursing mothers can change and feed their babies. While the inaugural site in Flatiron served as a testbed for the concept, both design aesthetic and programme were defined with the launch of the second New York space, in SoHo. Occupying a converted loft off Mercer Street, The Wing

Fig 5.4.3 and 5.4.4 Different seating areas accommodate different types of activity. Furniture is designed to be ergonomic in every space, so that members can work anywhere they choose

SoHo opened in 2017, before doubling in size two years later. The space is characterised by features that have since been repeated in most of the other locations, including arched doorways and bookshelves organised by colour. It also includes a fitness room and a daycare centre, The Little Wing.

Designing for inclusivity

The designers responsible for The Wing's look and feel are architect Alda Ly and interior designer Chiara de Rege, who collaborated on the first six locations before the company set up an in-house design team. Ly and de Rege helped The Wing build an identity that is instantly recognisable. Spaces feel luxurious but also bright and airy, with vibrant colours, curved shapes and plush fabrics. 'It wasn't about being girly-girl,' explains de Rege. 'We wanted it to be productive for work but without feeling like a gentleman's club.'

The visual style of the interiors was designed to reflect the varying tastes of its founders; Gelman loves Memphis design and mid-century furniture, while Kassan's style is more bohemian and eclectic. This translates into a diverse mix of furniture styles, with vintage pieces accompanying the bespoke designs. Colour palettes vary between locations, but there is one shade that features in them all – millennial pink, the blush tone that became a global trend around the same time The Wing first opened. Its popularity stems from being considered less gendered than other pinks, making it an appropriate choice for a space aiming to combine femininity with inclusivity. However, de

Rege chose it for other reasons. 'We weren't thinking, this is a women's space, let's use the colour pink,' she explains. 'I find that certain pinks are good neutrals that can go with lots of other colours.' At SoHo, the shade is paired with pastel hues inspired by the Italian Riviera, including baby blue, ochre yellow and rose gold. 'It makes the space a bit warmer,' adds de Rege. Other details contain more deliberate references to femininity, from custom wallpapers that reference famous women in New York's history, to meeting rooms named after famous female characters like Lara Croft and Charlotte Pickles.

A functional workplace

Underlying the stylistic elements are practical solutions that make The Wing's spaces functional as well as Instagram-pretty. Before designing SoHo, de Rege spent days at the Flatiron location observing how facilities were occupied. She noticed that laptops were typically used everywhere, in the lounge and cafe areas as well as desk spaces, so adjustments were made to the proportions of built-in seats and surfaces at SoHo to make them comfortable enough for a full day of work. Taller surfaces allow members to use a laptop while standing, while small C-shaped tables make it easier to work from a sofa. 'We realised how important programming was to these locations,' says the designer. 'We had to make sure that furniture was ergonomically correct for people working during the day, but also flexible, so that when, say 250 people come to hear Senator Gillibrand speak, everything can be moved around.' Room sizes were also adapted

Fig 5.4.5 A cafe space called The Perch is designed to feel welcoming, with soft pink hues, terrazzo tables, wooden surfaces and brass details

based on use patterns from Flatiron. The SoHo cafe is much larger, reflecting its importance to members as a meeting space, while the beauty room is smaller, as it only gets busy at certain times. And like all Wing sites, the thermostat is set at 23°C in every room to reflect women's higher temperature needs.

The Wing has many obstacles to overcome in order to rebuild its reputation, but it still stands as a model for how workplaces can cultivate new forms of community. Through interior design, it seeks to tell a different story to the one being told in the media, expressing the spirit of openness and optimism that the company was founded on.

Case study: The Department Store

Operator/Client: Squire & Partners

Architect/Interior designer: Squire & Partners

Type: Private office and co-working in converted department store

Location: London, UK

Completion year: 2017

Gross internal floor area: 6,147sqm

As the workplace of London-based architect Squire & Partners, The Department Store shows how a company headquarters can capture the spirit of co-working,

promoting a culture of collaboration. Housed in a rehabilitated department store in Brixton, its interiors draw on the practice's experience of designing workspaces, as well as lessons learned over the years about the creative power of collectivity. With flexible facilities and varied events, the building opens up to both the design industry and the local community in all kinds of ways.

Fig 5.5.1 and 5.5.2 As well as fixed desks, there are informal meeting spaces dotted through the office floors, where staff collaborate with others, or simply take time out from the computer

Squire & Partners had previously occupied an office in King's Cross but, after 16 years, had outgrown it. One thing had become particularly clear over that time: having more space made the practice more creative. Every time a new facility was added or an existing one was expanded, the attitude and productivity of staff would increase, whether it was expanding the model shop, or opening a bar and restaurant in the warehouse next door. Everyone was keen to avoid an office with too much emphasis on the antisocial computer, rather than on the more communicative aspects of being a designer, like pinning up drawings for group discussion or critique. They even found that inviting clients to work in their reception would lead to interesting conversations and ideas. 'We knew we couldn't work well sitting at one desk,' explains partner Tim Gledstone. 'We work better when we are communicating with others, encouraging clients to come and meet us rather than going to them, and by having a level of hospitality.'

A centre of creativity

Containing over 6,000sqm, the former Bon Marché department store was three times the size of space that the practice had been looking for. But instead of treating this as a negative, Squire & Partners saw it

as an opportunity to create a more generous offering. Ground floor spaces are rented out to businesses with a community focus: a record shop for a local vinyl brand, a post office, a coffee roastery and a restaurant with co-working facilities. Other spaces in The Department Store are used by the architects but designed with sharing in mind, in a way that makes them more financially viable and efficient.

Among them is the 300sqm basement space, Downstairs. The company needed a place to hold team meetings once a week, for more than 200 staff. It made no sense to create a space that would sit vacant six days a week, nor to regularly hire a room elsewhere; the obvious solution was to create a space with the flexibility to suit this function and multiple others. Folding furniture and large storage areas allow the basement to quickly transform into a venue for exhibitions, talks or parties, during events like London Design Festival or Black History Month. It hosts yoga classes twice a week, and one or two community events every month, turning it into a space of constant activity.

Similarly, a huge model-making workshop makes sense in the context of sharing. Equipped with cutting-edge technology, including CNC routers, laser cutters, 3D printers and a vast assortment of tools, these rooms can be opened up to other local designers, makers and businesses, and used to host educational workshops and demonstrations.

Fig 5.5.3 (Top) A flexible basement space is used for company meetings, but also hosts exhibitions, talks and events. Flexible furniture and lighting ensure it is fully adaptable

Fig 5.5.4 An extensive model-making facility is another space that is designed for sharing. Other designers and creatives are known to host workshops here

Encouraging interaction

Squire & Partners' workspaces are organised over the building's first, second and third floors. Much like The Ministry, a co-working space that the firm created for Ministry of Sound, these floors are organised to encourage staff to move around. As well as fixed desks, there are meeting areas dotted all over the space to allow people to easily break away. 'A key thing is finding that balance between individuality and collectivism,' says Gledstone. 'You can't just be open-plan and you can't be in rabbit hutches. You need really good circulation and you need genuine social space, which is often the problem with bad co-working spaces. It needs to be comfortable.'

A newly built fourth floor contains a restaurant and bar, Upstairs, which is open throughout the day and into the evening, for staff and anyone else who pays for a membership. It operates a strict laptop-free rule during the day, making it a place for conversation rather than isolation. This is signalled by extensive glazing on both sides and overhead, and a mix of large group seating areas inside and out. It brings people together throughout the day, but also encourages them to spend time together after hours and at the weekends.

Fig 5.5.5 A no-laptop rule is enforced in the top-floor restaurant, which is open to staff and members. It becomes both a meeting place and social space, open into the evenings

A recipe for success

Having worked on numerous projects turning large rundown buildings into offices, Gledstone believes there is a distinct formula for creating workspaces that users want to buy into, in terms of aesthetics and functionality. Alongside basic characteristics like high ceilings and good access to daylight and ventilation, he suggests that staircases can be key. 'It's surprising how important it is to have a big grand staircase, rather than one in the armpit of a building,' he states.

Character should be present but not overbearing, so there are still opportunities for personalisation. In The Department Store, this comes through the pairing of historic details, from tiled floors to graffiti murals, with adaptable display spaces such as shelving units and pin-up boards. Scale must also be managed, with no more than 10 people per space. 'It's more like working in a Cluedo house than it is one giant ballroom,' adds Gledstone.

There are lifestyle benefits here too. Cycle storage and shower facilities make it easy for staff to fit other activities around their work lives, such as going to the gym. With London rents continuing to rise, Squire & Partners acknowledges that for some, these showers are likely to be better than the ones they have at home. That makes them a valuable asset.

The recent addition of The Department Store Studios, a five-storey extension at the rear of the building, introduces co-working to the mix. Offering both desks for rent and more informal areas, it means that Squire & Partners can now offer long-term workspaces for like-minded companies. Given the facilities available, these spaces have a lot to offer small architecture and design studios who, for instance, can't afford their own model shops. In turn, they offer the practice even more opportunities for cross-fertilisation.

There is no reason why this approach couldn't be adopted by other companies looking to reap the benefits of collectivity.

Fig 5.5.6a Ground floor plan

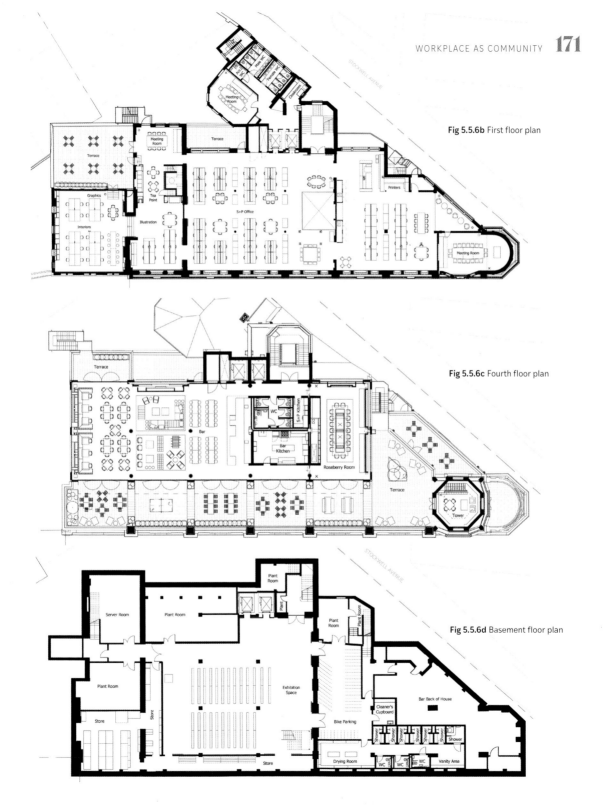

Fig 5.5.6b First floor plan

Fig 5.5.6c Fourth floor plan

Fig 5.5.6d Basement floor plan

Fig 6.0.0 Hotel rooms takes the form of 'smart lofts' at Zoku Amsterdam by Concrete, 2016

6.
The work–life merge

Working from home

The year 2020 will go down in history as the world's largest work-from-home experiment. As a result of the COVID-19 pandemic, working from home became the new normal for many. In the UK, the number of us working within the confines of our domestic spaces during the initial lockdown period represented 47% of the nation's active workforce, with similar patterns observed in other countries.[1] That's a surprisingly high figure considering that a significant proportion of the UK workforce were furloughed at this time, so weren't able to work at all.

For freelancers, this wasn't a radical shift; working from home was already the default choice for the majority. The real change was felt by companies, many of which had in the past been reluctant to let their staff work away from the office. Faced with this new reality, many realised the benefits of a more flexible setup, for both them and their employees. Although certain tasks required colleagues to be physically together, there were also plenty that could be carried out more efficiently away from the distractions of the busy workplace. As a result, remote or semi-remote working is now a permanent option for many who previously had

Fig 6.0.1 Located 90 minutes' drive from Berlin, Coconat is a co-living venue in a former hotel. Billed as a 'workation retreat', it offers space for individuals and groups to focus on work projects

no other choice but to commute to an office every day. We may yet see working from home become the new normal for good.

In the past, a home-working setup typically involved a room designated as a study, where piles of papers could be kept alongside the necessary heavy-duty items like the desktop computer, the telephone and the printer. With the uptake of mobile devices, not to mention rising property prices, the study became seen as a thing of the past, effectively replaced by the dining table, the sofa or even the bed. It's no coincidence that the bed overtook the sofa as the most used piece of furniture in British homes in 2016.[2] For those less keen on having their work and home life completely merge, there is a middle ground to be found. New residential models are finding ways to integrate workspaces into home environments, but to make them far more flexible than the study ever was.

For large-scale student housing, co-living and build-to-rent models, the solution is fairly simple. The private living space should include some area for focused solo work, which can be fairly modest; a small desk within another room can suffice. At the same time, they provide a dedicated co-working facility where residents can work alongside others. In some cases, this can be a place for scheduled group events, workshops and discussions. The problem becomes more complex when dealing with smaller properties, but not impossible to navigate. As our case study Garden House shows, a co-working area can just be an extra living space in the home, used for work by day and other activities in the evenings.

We're all becoming digital nomads

'In the future we will all be homeless.' These were the words of James Scott, former COO of The Collective, describing the concept of co-living at a technology festival in 2016. He was trying to grab people's attention, sure, but the point behind the message was compelling. With increased mobility and a reduced desire to settle down, we're gradually decoupling the function of living from a single physical location. By moving from a model of subscription homes, it's possible to take this idea even further. If home ownership is no longer a goal, you can minimise the number of possessions you own, making it easy to move between homes, cities and even countries on a regular basis.

People who live this kind of lifestyle are usually referred to as digital nomads. They are understood to be people who travel the world, but unlike traditional backpackers, they are working professionals. Thanks to mobile devices, they are able to carry out their work in any location, providing it has electrical power and a wifi connection. In the past, digital nomads would typically live between hotels and hostels, and work in coffee shops and public libraries. But now, with the introduction of co-living and co-working, these individuals can enjoy more of the same comforts they would in a traditional home or workplace, and feel like they belong to a community. That makes the package a whole lot more attractive, allowing this model to move from being something radical and niche, to an aspirational lifestyle choice. Today's digital nomad doesn't necessarily have to be a world traveller. They could be someone who uses co-living to help them divide

Fig 6.0.2 and 6.0.3 Eden Locke Edinburgh puts a new spin on the long-stay hotel model. Designed by Grzywinski+Pons, it aims to combine the comfort of an Airbnb property with the style of a hotel

their time between two or three locations, as they juggle work and family life. Or it might be someone with a fixed address, but who spends several weeks or months a year in other locations, using Airbnb as a way to cover their rent or mortgage while they're away.

There are a number of co-live/co-work models designed specifically with the digital nomad in mind, like our case studies Outpost and Mokrin House. In cities, the dated model of the long-stay hotel has been replaced by more flexible accommodation that blurs the line between hotel and home. There are also examples of co-living in rural locations and holiday destinations, selling the concept of the 'workation'. They promise spaces where guests can focus on projects, away from the distractions of the city, but separated from tourists who are only interested in having a good time.

The main obstacle these projects face is affordability – the concept is only feasible if you can make it work at residential prices, rather than hotel rates. That's not the case for most of our case studies, but there's no reason why it couldn't be for future examples. As with all forms of residential design, we can expect to see more diversity of budgets emerge in this sector as it develops further. Rob Wagemans, who designed our co-living-style hotel case study Zoku, believes the nomadic lifestyle has already become a goal for many, including himself. 'Instead of buying a house in the Hamptons or in the Amsterdam countryside, I'd prefer to own three little Zokus: one in Cape Town, one in New York and one in London,' he says. 'It's probably more affordable than having one big house in the countryside and it means that I'm a truly mobile citizen.' We'll soon see whether he's right.

Case study: Garden House

Operator/Client: Noiascape

Architect/Interior designer: Teatum+Teatum

Type: Rented co-living in converted house

Location: London, UK

Completion year: 2017

Gross internal floor area: 99sqm

Garden House offers a form of co-living that feels familiar, but is quietly radical. Through a series of considered interventions, this simple terraced house in west London allows two to four people to comfortably live and work together. On the surface it is just like any shared house, containing a mix of private rooms and communal spaces. But unlike most properties of its size, it allows all of its residents to work from home, without the drawbacks that – thanks to the coronavirus lockdowns – many have become familiar with. Separate floors for work life and home life allow the two to effectively coexist without fear of overlap, while a visually open layout helps to reduce feelings of isolation.

A shift in the market

The design developed out of a research project by architects Tom and James Teatum. As well as running their practice, Teatum+Teatum Architects, the pair also

Fig 6.1.1 Garden House contains multifunctional living spaces, so that activities like eating, working and socialising can coexist

Fig 6.1.2 A loft-like room on the second floor offers a place for residents to work from home, which is visually connected to the level below

have a property company, Noiascape, developing and renting homes they have designed. As landlords, they began to notice a shift in what people wanted from their living spaces, parallelled by the rise of mobile devices, and they wanted to see whether architecture could offer an answer. A survey revealed that, excluding sleep, their tenants were typically spending just 17% of their time at home, even in properties of 50–100sqm. Freelance workers, needing only a laptop and a wifi connection, would still often opt to work elsewhere. It seemed the key to making spaces more usable had nothing to do with size.

The solution proposed by Garden House is to make living spaces more ambiguous, facilitating different patterns of use. Rooms are not defined by function – there is no dining room, no lounge – as this merely limits their potential. 'People don't want to work in their living room or their bedroom,' explains Tom Teatum. 'They want a space where they can feel comfortable, a fluid space for everything from eating to working to socialising, but it has to be able to do all of those things in parallel.' Here, these various activities are accommodated in two spaces with distinct characters: on the first floor, a generous room is designed for cooking, eating and socialising, while on the second floor, a more intimate space is better suited to working or reading. However,

Fig 6.1.3 and 6.1.4 Inbuilt joinery creates spaces where people can spend time alone, but also interact with others. A staircase integrates a bookcase and window seat, creating opportunities to stop and linger

with laptops and tablets easy to move around, the two can easily swap roles: for instance, on a summer's evening some residents might want to spend time together on the second floor roof terrace, while another might stay on the first floor to finish off some work. Meanwhile, there are two bedrooms and bathrooms on the lower level, designed to suit either couples or singles.

The value of visual connectivity

For a feeling of fluidity, visual connections are maintained between floors. A see-through bridge made from perforated metal links the two living spaces, while a large internal window allows anyone working on the top floor to observe the comings and goings of those below. Even the bedrooms have sliding pocket doors so they don't always have to be private. This means there are moments where it is possible to look right across or right through the building. In this way, residents can feel comfortably alone in a space but still feel connected to other things going on in the building.

'Our thinking has been very much informed by the way people behave when they go to a pub,' says Teatum. 'There's something about those types of spaces, which are public but can feel very private, that needs to be brought forward into this typology. You can be happy sitting there on your own, reading a magazine, but you could also, very casually, engage with other people.' In Garden House, custom furniture helps to facilitate the same kinds of informal interactions. A staircase integrates a bookshelf and window seat, inviting you to stop and linger, while a bench seat creates a secluded corner spot, perfect for observing activity without necessarily taking part.

These integrated joinery elements have other benefits too. They make it possible for residents to move in without bringing any of their own furniture, meaning those only planning to stay for a year or two don't need to invest in objects they'll likely get rid of at the end of their tenancy. This setup suits a more nomadic approach to living that is especially common in young people. At the same time, these inbuilt furniture pieces allow people to easily make spaces their own. Shelves and ledges create places for displaying objects or hanging artworks. 'One thing we've recognised in rental properties is that, as soon as people enter, they very quickly want to colonise them with their own objects,' explains Teatum. 'We obviously don't want people putting holes in the walls, so lots of spaces are designed so that a postcard, a print or a photo can be displayed on a surface.'

Engaging with the public

The only thing missing from Garden House, according to its architects, is a public element. In their latest project, High Street House, the pair have applied the same ideas to a 12-bedroom block, above a retail unit that can also be used for co-working and exhibitions. This project uses economies of scale to give residents even more opportunities for engagement. Together, these two projects hint at a future where the concept of home is expanded beyond the idea of a singular, enclosed unit, to one that includes a vibrant mix of private, semi-public and public spaces. It is a future where home and workplace can be both together and separate, and give something back to local communities.

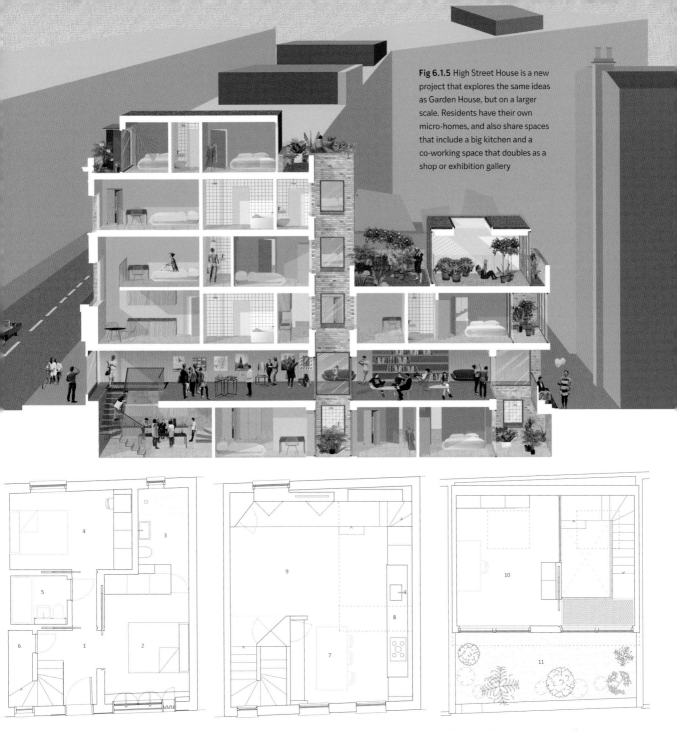

Fig 6.1.5 High Street House is a new project that explores the same ideas as Garden House, but on a larger scale. Residents have their own micro-homes, and also share spaces that include a big kitchen and a co-working space that doubles as a shop or exhibition gallery

ig 6.1.6a Garden house, ground floor plan

Fig 6.1.6b Garden house, first floor plan

Fig 6.1.6c Garden house, second floor plan

Case study: Zoku Amsterdam

Operator: Zoku

Architects: Concrete, Mulderblauw

Interior designer: Concrete

Type: Hotel/Residential hybrid and co-working in converted office block

Location: Amsterdam, the Netherlands

Completion year: 2016

Gross internal floor area: 5,800sqm

Describing itself as a 'work-meets-play hotel', Zoku Amsterdam combines the concepts of hotel, home and workplace into a single building. Revolutionising the outdated aparthotel concept, it offers 133 rooms where individuals can comfortably stay for three days, three months or even three years. There are spaces to work,

socialise and relax, used by people based in Amsterdam as well as those travelling through, and a programme of activities that encourage people to get to know their neighbours and surroundings.

Zoku's target audience is the digital nomad, a new breed of travelling professional who travels light and isn't bound by location-specific forms of employment. 'We see personal and professional lifestyles changing, boundaries between work and leisure fading, and borders blurring as people become more mobile than ever,' reads the mission statement written by Zoku founders Hans Meyer and Marc Jongerius. In it, the pair set out their vision for a complete hybrid of the hotel and serviced-apartment models, promoting balanced lifestyles, and fostering physical connections

Fig 6.2.1 In Zoku's 'smart lofts', the bed is raised up on a platform out of the way. This allows the space to be used for a variety of home and work activities

Fig 6.2.2 and 6.2.3 See-through shelving units loosely divide the open-plan 'living room' space. Furniture facilitates conversations: for instance, there are sofas that bend in the middle

Fig 6.2.4 Instead of a restaurant, there is an open kitchen where diners communicate directly with the chef. Long tables and benches encourage people to chat to each other

as well as digital ones. 'The nature of a hotel has always been a place where people from different nationalities, backgrounds and fields of expertise stay together. However they rarely met and interacted,' it reads. 'We saw the potential of stretching the definition of a hotel into a place where people can stay for longer periods and truly engage with the world and people around them.'

Reimagining the long-stay hotel

For creative direction, Meyer and Jongerius looked to Rob Wagemans, founder of Amsterdam-based architecture and interiors studio Concrete. Meyer and Wagemans had previously teamed up on CitizenM, the hotel brand that offers affordable luxury to the 'mobile citizen' with the use of modular construction.

With Zoku, they have developed this idea even further, creating a design for 'smart lofts' that could be inserted inside disused office buildings. More like micro-apartments than bedroom suites, these adaptable spaces accommodate other activities besides sleeping – they can just as easily serve as meeting rooms or social lounge spaces – yet some of them are no bigger than 24sqm. Accompanying the lofts are a diverse mix of communal spaces, designed to stimulate casual encounters in the most relaxed way possible. Instead of a restaurant, an open kitchen filled with big tables encourages diners to chat to the chef and each other. There is a workshop space equipped with everything from tools to games, a shop selling groceries, and various locations where it's possible to make a cup of coffee or pour yourself a beer.

'We've tried to create a neighbourhood,' explains Wagemans. 'In every hotel you're anonymous. You have a room number and you never know who's next to you. In Zoku, we hope to stimulate you to know who's on the other side of the street – the street being the corridor – and to share knowledge and friendship.' These interplays aren't just reserved for people staying in the building, either. Although the social spaces are not open to the general public, it is possible to become a member or pay for a day pass, and occupants are encouraged to invite guests. The intention is not to be exclusive, but to build a community of like-minded people.

A home from home

The building reinforces this idea in its layout, which places social spaces at the very top. A plant-filled greenhouse on the sixth floor serves as an arrival space, creating a notable departure from the busy entrance on Weesperstraat. This leads through to the 'living room', an open-plan space loosely divided up into zones by a series of open shelving units. A mix of different seating types facilitate quiet study, one-on-one conversations or group meetups. Sofas bend in the middle, so that people can easily face one another, and some spaces offer more privacy than others. The room is also filled with plants, cushions, candles, lighting and other curiosities. Wagemans describes it as curated chaos. 'I think chaos helps you to focus, helps you to meet other people and helps you to feel at home,' he says. 'It shouldn't feel like a design space; no one's home feels like that.'

Four different colour schemes feature in the living room, as well as other communal areas that include a games room, various bookable meeting spaces and a subdividable events room. Spaces with a domestic character feature natural colours and soft materials, to create a sense of calm, while locations with a more ambient mood are embellished with plants and green tones. In spots where guests can enjoy the start or end of a day, shades of red and orange emulate the warm hues of sunrise and sunset, while workspaces feature denim textiles and matching indigo shades, representing the uniform of the freelance worker (jeans, rather than a suit). Where different moods overlap, colours mix together, contributing to the busy aesthetic.

A room that does more

In the lofts, the design centres around space-efficiency. These rooms are organised vertically as well as horizontally, taking advantage of the generous ceiling heights typical of office buildings. The bed is raised on a platform, accessed by retractable stairs, leaving the rest of the room free for other activities. As Wagemans points out, 'it's the only hotel in the world where the bed is not the most prominent factor in your room'. There's a table with room for four, a lounge corner with a sofa, and a functional kitchenette. A study desk slots into an alcove beneath the bed, while a bathroom fits in behind the kitchen, and both are framed by storage closets. There are even gymnastics hoops hanging from the ceiling.

Clever details make these rooms easy to adapt and customise. Furniture can be moved around, and both the bedroom and the study space can be screened off. A steel U-beam runs around the walls so that guests can pin up their own photos or postcards with magnets, or display

Fig 6.2.5 and 6.2.6 Workshops and meeting rooms cater for different work–life activities, but also serve other functions. There's a cabinet full of tools, including a 3D printer, and a variety of games

their choice of framed artworks (there's a swapping station on each floor, offering plenty of options). For those only staying a short time, filling the fridge can be enough to make the space feel homely. 'It may be that it has nothing to do with stuff but with behaviour,' says Wagemans. 'If you bake your own egg in the morning and eat it in your own room, it feels like a house rather than a bedroom.'

Zoku is a clever example of how working and living nomadically can become very normal. It suggests that a transient lifestyle can still include home comforts and meaningful face-to-face interactions, whether that's dining with a stranger or bumping into a friend abroad. Zoku Amsterdam has a list of testimonials from people who have met clients and collaborators in its spaces, or used its facilities to kickstart a business. With new locations opening in Vienna, Copenhagen, Brussels, Paris and more, that list looks set to grow.

Case study: Mokrin House

Operator: Mokrin House

Client: Terra Panonica

Architect/Interior designer: Autori

Type: Co-working retreat on renovated estate

Location: Mokrin, Serbia

Completion year: 2011–2014

Gross internal floor area: 1,871sqm

In a remote village in north Serbia, a formerly rundown estate is now a live/work destination for digital nomads. Combining co-living and co-working, Mokrin House is a place where both individuals and groups from around the world come to pursue creative projects, build relationships and improve their wellbeing, away from the distractions of the city. In a mix of refurbished and contemporary buildings, there are purpose-built facilities for workshops, lectures and quiet study, areas that stimulate social interactions and personal growth, and space for up to 40 people to stay. These versatile spaces bring visitors together with the local community, helping to create business opportunities for a region suffering widespread social and economic decline.

A model that evolved organically

The estate consists of five buildings around a landscaped courtyard. Located within Mokrin village, it is a peaceful and idyllic site, surrounded by trees. It was this setting that attracted entrepreneur Branimir Brkljač

Fig 6.3.1 Mokrin House consists of five co-live and co-work buildings surrounding a landscaped courtyard

Fig 6.3.2 and 6.3.3 Buildings are designed to encourage people inside, with glazed doors, full-height windows and spacious entrance decks

to buy the property back in 2009. Neither co-working nor co-living were in Brkljač's mind at this point. Having grown up in the area but spending most of his adult life abroad, he was simply looking to find a place close to family and friends where he could host events. But when young architecture studio Autori proposed upgrading the estate with modern buildings, Brkljač started to see greater potential. 'Migration from rural to urban areas has been pretty significant in this part of the world over the last 30 or 40 years; lots of villages are vacant,' he explains. 'These kinds of projects can re-energise rural areas, so that was something that really motivated me.'

Without a clear idea of precisely how the buildings would be used, both design and construction progressed slowly over the course of six years. Due to the remote location, nearly three hours' drive from Belgrade, the Autori team spent a lot of this time living and working onsite. This became a catalyst for other emerging artists and designers to come to Mokrin House to work, and the property naturally evolved into a hub of creativity. At the same time, co-working was gaining traction as a global trend. Brkljač realised he had created the perfect setup to bring the co-working model to the countryside.

Catering for both locals and tourists

Mokrin House is like a rural holiday retreat, except that it prioritises work over leisure. Its business model is built around two major groups of users. The first are the so-called digital nomads. In this case, they tend to be overseas travellers who are often moving between countries, staying for weeks or months at a time. The second group are companies based in Serbia or neighbouring countries, who come for a few days to host team-building activities for their employees. Mokrin House also offers free use of its co-working facilities to village residents, to support the local economy. This mix helps to maintain a base level of activity throughout the year, so the place doesn't feel deserted outside the peak summer season.

Mokrin House's architecture is designed to appear open and welcoming in both its layout and details. There is a natural centre of activity, thanks to the courtyard arrangement, and buildings encourage people to venture in with fully glazed doors and generous entrance decks. There are also secluded corners, like the swimming pool, and seating areas dotted among the trees. 'You get the feeling that it's your place, not just your room and not just your desk,' says Brkljač. 'The whole place is your place.' This is essential, he claims, in building the sense of community needed for a place like Mokrin House to function. It is even more important here than in the city, as people who come to Mokrin will be spending the majority of their time in this single place with the same group of people. It has to offer a level of service that suits everyone's working routines, however irregular. 'Some people work during the nights, others during the day, but whenever they are out of that working schedule we want to make it easy for them to find activities,' Brkljač says.

Fig 6.3.4 and 6.3.5 Rooms are designed to be multifunctional, like this events/dining space, with adjustable projection screens that double as space dividers, and a rotating table with integrated sink

To accommodate this level of flexibility, many spaces are designed to be multifunctional, particularly in the co-working buildings known as House B, House C and House D. Rooms here include a meeting room that doubles as an exhibition gallery or yoga studio, and an events space that transforms into a huge dining room, thanks to a projection screen that hides the kitchen. 'We added another layer,' says Branislav Ristović, an architect at Autori. 'It's co-working with a twist.' A first-floor terrace creates a sheltered, open-air space for working or dining, while the courtyard is also used for film screenings and sports. Autori even designed bespoke furniture pieces to support multiple uses, including a wooden bench made from recycled wooden baulks and a rotating table with an integrated sink.

Quality in design

The design aesthetic throughout Mokrin House is deliberately clean and minimal. In a village where modern architecture is a rarity, the approach was not to shout too loud. The industrial feel of the metal structures is softened by the abundance of windows and skylights, stark white walls and the addition of wooden joinery elements. Plants also play a big role, particularly on House 23, one of the two co-living buildings, where a lattice facade encourages vines to grow up the walls. The other co-living building, House A, is the only exception. This renovated property, which was originally the estate's main house, has a more bold, eclectic feel. Patterned wallpapers are paired with retro furniture and lighting, referencing different periods across the building's 100-year history.

Brkljač believes that architecture and design is one of the reasons why guests keep returning to Mokrin House: that the estate offers them the same level of quality they can find in a city, coupled with the luxury of having nature all around. The project is certainly a compelling model for how co-working can transform rural areas as well as urban ones. It is predicted that more than two-thirds of the global population will be living in cities by 2050 – an estimated 6.7 billion people – while rural areas will continue to decline.[3] Projects like Mokrin House could help to change the fortunes of some of these regions.

Fig 6.3.6 The design aesthetic is clean and minimal. The industrial aesthetic of the metal structures is softened by white surfaces, wooden joinery and an abundance of windows

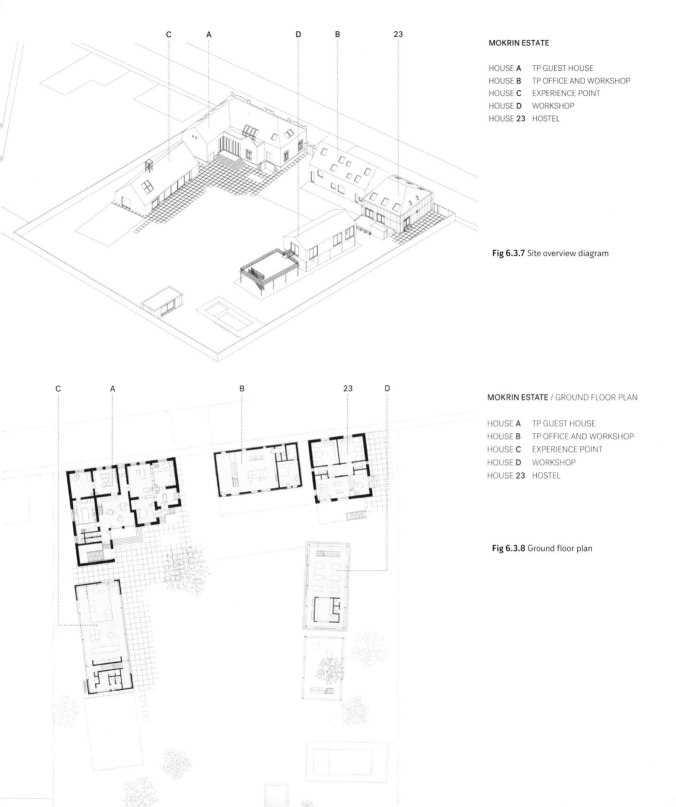

MOKRIN ESTATE

HOUSE **A**   TP GUEST HOUSE
HOUSE **B**   TP OFFICE AND WORKSHOP
HOUSE **C**   EXPERIENCE POINT
HOUSE **D**   WORKSHOP
HOUSE **23**   HOSTEL

Fig 6.3.7 Site overview diagram

MOKRIN ESTATE / GROUND FLOOR PLAN

HOUSE **A**   TP GUEST HOUSE
HOUSE **B**   TP OFFICE AND WORKSHOP
HOUSE **C**   EXPERIENCE POINT
HOUSE **D**   WORKSHOP
HOUSE **23**   HOSTEL

Fig 6.3.8 Ground floor plan

Case study: Outpost Ubud Penestanan

Operator: Outpost

Architect: Alexis Dornier

Type: Co-working retreat in converted residential

Location: Bali, Indonesia

Completion year: 2020

Gross internal floor area: 1,750sqm

This co-working retreat in Bali challenges the notion that nomadic lifestyles are just for the young. Outpost Ubud Penestanan is a combined co-living and co-working venue that doesn't just attract people in their twenties and thirties, but also many in their forties, fifties and sixties. It reinvents the backpacker experience for working professionals, in an environment that models itself on the youth hostel but has a more grown-up approach. As well as vacations and adventures (the obvious attractions of the location), it offers opportunities to concentrate on work, learn new skills and build a network. Guests come for weeks or months at a time, either for a working retreat or as part of a full-time travelling lifestyle.

'There are three main values that our members have,' explains David Abraham, who co-founded the Outpost brand with partner Bryan Stewart. 'They want to explore the world, they want to grow personally and professionally, and they want to connect with other people and places.'

Adapting to transient lifestyles

Ubud Penestanan is the company's fourth venue, following other locations in Bali and Cambodia. It comprises three buildings that were originally apartment blocks before a series of renovations by Alexis Dornier, a German architect who has been based in Bali since 2013. Before being taken over by Outpost, the blocks were first converted into a 24-room hotel, then used by another co-living operator, Roam Living.

Dornier's most significant alteration came in the initial conversion; he transformed the rooftops of all three two-storey blocks into social spaces, which are linked by bridges and sheltered beneath steel-framed canopies. In the co-living setup these spaces become crucial in creating a sense of community. In the current layout they include workspaces and meeting rooms, a restaurant and lounge, and a flexible yoga and meditation space that can also host events. Down below, a ground level courtyard offers a more informal vibe, with a swimming pool, a terrace and a kitchen where guests can prepare their own meals in company. Bedrooms are located on the ground and first floors, and there are 24 in total.

Abraham and Stewart designed the Outpost model around their own experiences of living and working between cities. Stewart in particular – whose work involved helping companies in developing countries find investment – found he spent very little time in the places he called home. Their vision was for a more transient form of residence, located away from hectic city life but still offering opportunities to spend

Fig 6.4.1 Outpost Ubud Penestanan consists of 24 co-living rooms organised around a courtyard, with a swimming pool in the centre and communal facilities on the roof

time with others. At the core of their business is an events programme that focuses on enterprise as well as leisure. There are workshops where you can learn about marketing skills or search-engine optimisation, as well as leisure activities like movie nights and social activities. These events are what drive guests to keep on coming back to Outpost, or to visit the company's other locations. 'When people come all the way out to Bali, they're shedding their friends, they're shedding their lifestyle and they're coming to an unfamiliar environment,' says Abraham. 'They could go to an Airbnb and get something that may be of more value, but they miss out on that supportive environment. The role of Outpost is really to fill that gap.'

Comfortable being communal

The design is deliberately stripped back, with a focus on functionality, comfort and wellbeing. A palette of natural tones and simple materials extends throughout, with elements of stone, wood, concrete and rattan. The main injection of colour comes from the abundant plant life, which includes high-grown bamboo, palms and climbers. Dornier describes these plants as the most important material in his design. The idea, he explains, is that spaces are 'anti-design', with more emphasis on content than style. 'There are a lot of spaces in Bali that are cute, chic and Instagrammable,' he says. 'People don't really work there, they go for other reasons. But this is a place where you can really concentrate.' In this spirit, the workspaces are air-conditioned to help guests stay focused in the tropical climate without breaking a sweat. The walls of these spaces are glazed, but they have some opening panels and can be shaded using rolling bamboo screens.

Fig 6.4.2 and 6.4.3 Workspaces occupy spaces on the rooftop. Glass walls allow these spaces to be air-conditioned, but bamboo adjustable shades offer relief from the sun

Visibility is an important aspect of every space. The courtyard layout and open rooftop spaces make it possible for guests to see what's going on around them, even just by opening up the door of their room. There are no closed corridors or dark corners. 'We like spaces that turn in on themselves, because you can see who else is there and not feel creepy about it,' says Abraham. 'You have your privacy and you also have something social.' But within this open layout, there are still moments of intimacy. Staircases and entrances are kept narrow, to encourage casual interactions, while seating areas offer a small amount of seclusion without being closed off. 'Before we took over, the roof was completely empty,' continues Abraham. 'You had to have a lot of people up there for it not to feel empty. We wanted it to still feel open and airy with the wonderful view, but closed off enough so you don't feel isolated if there are not many people there.'

Fig 6.4.4 An open rooftop space is dedicated to yoga and meditation, but can also be used to host event A steel canopy, supported by V-shaped columns, provides shade

Reconnecting with nature

The digital nomad lifestyle was already on the rise before COVID-19 swept the world. While the pandemic has heightened people's fears about travel and interactions with strangers, it has also transformed the culture of remote working from a growing trend into a global phenomenon, not just for freelancers but also for those in employment. Outpost shows how non-urban locations might respond to this shift, creating hubs of productivity and entrepreneurship. Here, business and social opportunities are there for the taking, but the jungle location also makes it easy to get away from others and reconnect with nature.

'We've just added 500 million people to this lifestyle,' says Abraham, 'but I don't believe that everyone is going to want to work in the same place that they live. Even for the most introverted, I don't think that would be totally fulfilling. They will soon find out that they can be somewhere else besides home, whether that's for two weeks, four weeks, six weeks or the whole year. We're here to support that.'

Fig 6.4.5 Social spaces include a communal kitchen fronting the swimming pool area, so that occupants can prepare their own meals in the company of others

Fig 7.0.0 Fosbury & Sons
Harmony, Antwerp, by
Going East, 2016

7.
Design toolkit

Design Toolkit

The terms co-living and co-working, as this book shows, are open to many interpretations. In truth, they are shorthand for the infinite ways we can live and work together, and are best considered as a framework for new ideas of how to live our lives collectively.

Here is a checklist to guide your thinking and help you develop new ideas:

THE BRIEF

KNOW WHO YOU ARE DESIGNING FOR

 The lexicon at the start of this book offers you a starting point to explore this evolving and multifaceted sector, but it's important to recognise that there are numerous iterations of shared living and working, and plenty of opportunities to invent new versions. The key is to understand the specific needs of your audience and be flexible in responding to them. If you're designing housing for seniors, that doesn't mean you can't find ways to engage younger people. If you're designing a workspace, that doesn't mean it can't also include elements you would more typically find in housing.

The shared space provides an opportunity to reinvent how people of different ages, genders, ethnicity and backgrounds can live and work together, striking a balance between individuality and collectivism.

FIRST PRINCIPLES

PUT COMMUNITY AT THE HEART OF THE DESIGN PROCESS

 When designing for groups of people who may not have exclusive financial ownership, but whose livelihoods and personal wellbeing are so deeply invested in a project, there is both a moral and a business case for a more 'bottom-up' approach. All evidence suggests that putting community at the heart of the design process produces the most effective and sustainable solutions for shared space.

At K9 Coliving (see Chapter 3), residents played a crucial role in planning the layout and contents of the building, working with a project manager rather than a designer. This process of co-creation gave residents personal responsibility for the impact on the collective, and stimulated a profound sense of commitment that did not depend on financial transaction.

However, the process doesn't have to be that radical. An easier way to maintain a creative dialogue with a building's future occupants is to host collaborative workshops and design surgeries over the course of the design process. The process needn't end when a project is complete, either – it's possible, and often advisable, to connect feedback from residents into an ongoing management and design strategy.

INTERIOR DESIGN IS INTRINSIC

Even if the design process is community-led, collaboration with building design professionals is essential, not least because building is a highly technical (and expensive!) business. A qualified and experienced delivery team will optimise opportunity and eliminate risk.

This team should include a professional interior designer at an early stage. The interior of a building is its most intimate interface, the plane at which a building is most intensely experienced day to day by its users – a critical factor in intensively used shared space. Just as the inside of a building is as implicit as the outside, so interior design is not an optional add-on, concerned solely with interior decoration.

Instead, interior design constitutes every decision that must be made concerning the performance of a structure's interior, starting with emotional, cultural and practical considerations that are developed into a spatial plan. Then, critically in the building process, situating utilities – power, light, water, drainage, temperature control – to comprehensively service that plan. Failure to thoroughly think through the end result before utility points have been agreed too often results in compromise.

LEARN FROM OTHER TYPOLOGIES

Many of the best co-live and co-work spaces take ideas from the hospitality industry. Hotels, restaurants, bars and even shops offer lessons for how we can create healthier and happier homes and workspaces. These typologies suggest new ways of dividing up our private and public spaces, and a completely different set of space standards. But there are also tricks to learn about legibility and navigation, and ways to better provoke and encourage interaction.

Many of the case studies in this book have reinterpreted hospitality in unique ways. NeueHouse Hollywood (see Chapter 5) uses food and beverage operations as a way to restructure the functionality and sociability of the workplace, while the architects of Garden House (see Chapter 6) took cues from the traditional English pub, a space that is public but can feel very private, to create new ways of experiencing shared living space.

The blending of typologies presents both challenges and opportunities. Applying the space standards of hotels to residential, for instance, offers a chance to think more creatively, but the system is also susceptible to abuse. If you are replacing private space with shared space, you must be confident that it improves the experience for occupants. The pandemic, which confined people to their homes for periods of lockdown, has shone new light on the conversation around space standards, in combination with the need to ensure that people have access to nourishing outdoor space.

Fig 7.0.1 The interior design of BaseCamp's student accommodation schemes is based on 25hours Hotel in Berlin, created by the same interior designer, Studio Aisslinger

SCALE: OPPORTUNITY AND RISK

In co-living and co-working spaces, economy of scale is a gift, creating opportunities for features that are only affordable as a result of them being shared. For example, many co-live and co-work spaces offer a fully equipped gym. At a co-living scheme as large as The Collective Canary Wharf (see Chapter 3), residents can enjoy a whole load more, including a swimming pool, a spa, a huge kitchen and cinema rooms.

Larger schemes, though, run the risk of being intimidating, the opposite of communal. British anthropologist Robin Dunbar has codified how human beings form relationships in hierarchical layers, making good friends with up to 50 people and best friends with up to just 15.[1] This presents a challenge for schemes where the number of occupants is in the hundreds, but which still seek to cultivate a sense of binding community. While it's often financially more sustainable to consolidate communal space into a single location, it may be preferable to create several smaller communal spaces dotted through a scheme, in an effort to make the community feel more accessible.

When this isn't possible, design can compensate through subdividing a space, creating different and distinct atmospheres through purpose, finish, lighting and floor and ceiling levels, and increasing the number of access and exit points to make each zone independent of the others. Strategies will be most effective if developed in close collaboration with not only potential residents but, more realistically, the team who will manage the building and the amenities hosted within.

ESSENTIAL INGREDIENTS: IT'S EMOTIONAL

CULTIVATE A SENSE OF OWNERSHIP

While some of the case studies featured in this book are owned by the occupants (typically the intergenerational schemes), most are not. Instead space, whether co-live or co-work, is rented. But a sense of ownership is extremely valuable, emotionally and financially, to all stakeholders. It is well documented that a sense of ownership in shared space is critical to a sense of wellbeing; that agency over the space we occupy inspires confidence and calm. And the feeling of ownership is not dependent on the fact of possession, but can be delivered through design.

Personalisation

Creating opportunities for personalisation is common to successful shared spaces, particularly co-living schemes. Some owners and operators will support residents in making

private spaces their own, by organising and managing decorating. Other operators agree to residents superficially customising their personal space, contingent on tenants restoring those spaces to their original condition at the end of a contract.

Noticeboards, pegboard walls and open shelving are among the most common means of facilitating self-expression. But it's possible to be more creative. At The Collective Canary Wharf (see Chapter 3), interactive artworks create more extravert opportunities, while The Project at Hoxton (see Chapter 2) has a communal kitchen where cabinet doors are painted in chalkboard paint, so students can regularly redecorate them.

Control

Decor is not the only way to evoke feelings of ownership. Localised lighting allows people to control the atmosphere of the immediate space they inhabit. And it's surprising how being able to help yourself to a drink – whether it's a mug of tea or coffee, or a beer – inculcates a sense of domain.

ENCOURAGE SOCIABILITY

One of the main reasons why people opt for co-living and co-working environments is because they want to interact with others and avoid loneliness. Depending on the size and the nature of the scheme, it's possible to create opportunities for engagement with those both inside and outside the building.

Staircases and corridors

 Connective circulation space presents a multitude of opportunities for a building's occupants to engage, with different interpretations. A grand staircase, with plenty of space to stop and chat, will often become a vibrant meeting place. Equally, intimate passageways can encourage casual interactions, as people negotiate one another. The importance is less to do with size, and much more about the appeal of the route.

Guest rooms

 While shared space presents instant companionship, members of any community are likely to have visitors and guests, and they need to be accommodated too. Some co-living schemes feature dedicated guest rooms for friends and family to stay in, while various co-working spaces offer the potential to take on more or less space at short notice.

Community space

 It's no good creating a strong community within a building if it's isolated from the wider community it belongs to. Creating spaces and facilities that can be shared with others offers yet another way to take advantage of economies of scale. The Department Store (see Chapter 5) shows how this can work in various ways. Its basement, used as for weekly company meetings, doubles as a space for exhibitions and events, while its boastfully large model workshop regularly hosts tutorials for guests.

SAFEGUARD PRIVACY WITHOUT ISOLATION

People who choose shared space in which to live and work do so because they want to be with other people. But for shared space to be successful, connections require careful treatment to preserve harmony. Privacy strengthens community; buildings need to be vibrant, living entities, but also protect occupants from uninvited intrusion.

Visual connections that minimise acoustic transmission are key to creating controlled opportunities for engagement. If you can see other people but you can't hear one another, this creates a degree of privacy without full isolation. We see examples of this in The Student Hotel and Chapter King's Cross (see Chapter 2), where soundproof glazing allows visibility of activity in adjacent space while isolating sound. The former uses it to prompt inspiration in study rooms, while the latter uses it to create a more social atmosphere in and around the gym.

A good strategy is to create multiple layers of privacy within the design. In multigenerational, multifamily house Caring Wood (see Chapter 4) there are four: bedrooms and en-suite bathrooms accommodate individuals; lounge spaces are occupied by different family units; shared cooking, dining and relaxation spaces are open to the extended family; and there are also events spaces for the public and guests. The same rules can apply to co-working too, as shown by Belgian operator Fosbury & Sons (see Chapter 5), which creates four different zones in its workplaces: one reasonably public for administrative tasks; one quiet, isolated space for focused work; one space for collaborative project work; and one relaxation space.

Small moments of privacy can also be inserted into more public areas with great success and sensitivity. In living environments, this could be a quiet enclosure where someone can find sanctuary to read a book, while in co-working it could be a booth for taking phone calls.

WELLBEING: CREATE A GOOD MOOD

 People who feel good, or at least feel OK about feeling bad sometimes, will create more successful communities. We are hardwired to react emotionally to our environment – a connection to our ancient instincts for self-preservation, and a phenomenon which provides exciting possibilities for enriching our emotional lives and therefore our relationships and the communities we create.

Fig 7.0.2 A phone box creates an option for privacy in the otherwise open-plan workspace at Big and Tiny Silver Lake in California

Fig 7.0.3 Upstairs, the bar and restaurant space on the top floor of The Department Store, has a no laptop policy. This ensures it is a space for face-to-face interactions only

Nature

The value to wellbeing of contact with nature, biophilia, was well recognised before the advent of the recent pandemic. With the risk of viral transmission very much decreased outdoors it is likely that habitable space outside, for work and leisure, will be increasingly desirable in a shared habitat.

If outdoor space is not realistic, lavish indoor planting will at least activate the same biophilic response. Zoku Amsterdam (see Chapter 6) deploys planting to dramatic effect in its rooftop greenhouse reception space; a joyful, verdant contrast to the grey concrete of the streets below.

Scent

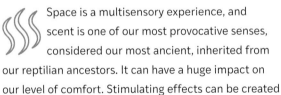

Space is a multisensory experience, and scent is one of our most provocative senses, considered our most ancient, inherited from our reptilian ancestors. It can have a huge impact on our level of comfort. Stimulating effects can be created in various ways, whether through introducing essential oils and flowers into a room, or allowing the smell of baking to filter out from the kitchen. It can also be damaging if not taken into consideration.

Screen-free zones

The corrosive effect of too much screen time on personal wellbeing and collective harmony is well documented. In shared space, a screen-free zone can be an appealing respite. The Project at Hoxton (see Chapter 2) features a small library where screens are banned, while the restaurant at The Department Store (see Chapter 5) is open to staff and members all day and evening, but never to screens. As a result, the types of interactions that take place in these spaces are markedly different than elsewhere.

ESSENTIAL INGREDIENTS: PRACTICALITIES

MAKE SPACE MULTIFUNCTIONAL

Flexibility is the common denominator of all successful shared space; multifunctionality means spaces can be used efficiently for the enjoyment and service of a wide community of people. But while ambiguity is desirable, aimlessness is not – the purpose needs to be clear, signalled through design, but open to interpretation.

Furniture

As we develop new types of live/work space, it's only natural that new types of furniture emerge. As we see in Flatmates (see Chapter 3), more complex designs for seating in particular can allow a living space to accommodate more diverse uses, and in some cases can allow multiple activities to take place simultaneously.

As furniture becomes more ambiguous, varying levels of comfort and privacy help to signpost different functional possibilities. High-back seating can create

Fig 7.0.4 Furniture is designed to be
moved around in the Flatmates co-living
project in Paris. The sofa is made up
of modular elements, and everything is
deliberately lightweight

seclusion, while curved seating helps to more easily facilitate face-to-face conversation. Meanwhile large, shared seats encourage interaction by physically bringing people together.

Versatility is key. A ping-pong table only has limited use, but if it doubles as a desk or dining table then it immediately becomes more purposeful. Ergonomics can also be subtly integrated into lounge furniture, meaning spaces designed for relaxation can also accommodate laptop use.

Space can be made especially flexible if different kinds of furniture can be stored, which is where folding and stacking elements come into play. If furniture can be easily and tidily stowed, then a lecture hall or meeting room can transform into an exhibition space or party venue. Adding castor wheels to furniture or other elements, such as partitions, facilities a similar level of adaptability. But wheels are not the only way to ensure furniture is mobile. Another option is to make objects purposely lightweight, so they're easy to lift.

Durability

 With mobility and metamorphoses comes the requirement that furniture be especially well made and of good quality, with any mechanisms designed to withstand heavy use. The same goes for internal finishes. Walls and surfaces need to be able to withstand regular contact, while flooring needs to be sufficiently smooth and robust to tolerate the drag of wheels and feet. Simple rubber or felt pads will protect floors and help furniture glide to different positions.

Power and lighting

 Flexibility and multifunctionality naturally require different lighting and power schemes, too. Layers of lighting circuits and simple dimmer switches can provide solutions. Our co-working case study NeueHouse Hollywood (see Chapter 5) solved the problem with manual lighting rigs, which are raised and lowered to create different moods, to suit different setups. Low-hanging pendant lights are great for creating a sultry mood, but should obviously be avoided where furniture is mobile!

With most people carrying electronics around with them these days – at the very least a smartphone – power points, particularly USB points, need to be well distributed, especially in a co-working space.

Storage

Well-designed storage is key to harmony in any building, but it's especially true in shared space, where the effect of personal possessions on companions needs to be controlled to avoid conflict. With that in mind, many co-living schemes offer storage lockers, usually for additional rent.

But perhaps the most essential storage requirement these days is for parcels. Internet sales and deliveries have been rising steadily, and during the pandemic they peaked at over 30% of all retail sales. Hanging rails will store dry-cleaning, and chilled storage – a chilled room or large fridge – will keep groceries fresh until collected.

Storage inside smaller private living space can be optimised with bespoke joinery; the rooms at BaseCamp Leipzig (see Chapter 2) are a good example of how limited personal space can provide generous storage if designed using customised furniture.

ACOUSTICS ARE CRITICAL

Sound can be critical when it comes to defining the difference between shared and private space. Many co-living and co-working schemes tackle this by grouping 'noisy' activities together; for instance, laundry rooms in many student housing projects are positioned alongside social spaces and games rooms, offering diversion from the tedium of waiting for laundry.

Materials can play a key role in an acoustic strategy, particularly when dealing with large spaces. Upholstered walls attenuate sound in student scheme Calico (see Chapter 2), while co-work building Big and Tiny Silver Lake (see Chapter 5) archives the same effect with cork boards, which double as pinboards.

But beware. In The Royal Hospital in London's Chelsea, home to British army veterans, residents complained that the place was too quiet after a high-quality renovation that included luxurious carpeting and curtains.

COMMUNITIES NEED TO COMMUNICATE

For a community to function well, it needs to establish functional methods of group communication, usually determined by scale and community purpose. Large, high-end co-work and co-live schemes might rely solely on a smartphone app. These vary in sophistication – some operate as a simple messaging service, while others integrate the ability to book shared services and facilities.

What's known as 'proptech', a portmanteau of property and technology, is increasingly expected in shared-space schemes, where an app can alert tenants to post or grocery deliveries or advertise social events. Here, it is likely the designer will be required to connect alerts with physical access and associated security.

Fig 7.0.5 At The Project at Hoxton, building signage includes space for listing events, helping to reinforce the feeling of community among the student residents

At a more low-tech level, a simple noticeboard can have great value, typically in a high-traffic zone. Simple doesn't have to mean ordinary – there's always scope for this to become a sculptural or characterful element, as this will probably encourage more people to contribute.

Without or without a noticeboard, physical signage of some sort is required across all shared schemes. The risk with superficially designed signage is that it can alienate people from a space, reminding them of a lack of familiarity, and therefore connection. The best kind of signage either intensifies the aesthetic qualities of a space or is intuitive. Colour can be used as a navigational tool, particularly in buildings where different floors look the same, and visual marker points can also help to create familiarity.

MOVING MORE REGULARLY

 Flexible tenancies can also mean more mobile tenants, so designers need to allow for more frequent moves in and out of a building. Some BTR schemes offer dedicated loading bays and service lifts for this purpose, preserving the fixtures, finishes and everyday function of the front-of-house space.

Moving needn't mean leaving, however; a mix of apartment types and/or workspaces in the same building means people can let their lives and work develop without changing address.

CARE AND REPAIR

 Designers need to make refuse disposal and recycling effortless for a community of occupants where civility is the lubricant of harmony. In some shared residential schemes, refuse chutes are included on each floor so tenants don't need to carry refuse too far through the building.

Repairs and maintenance are required on all buildings. In a BTR scheme like Angel Gardens (see Chapter 4), services like this are included, while on co-living schemes, caring for where you live is an opportunity to nurture connection and a sense of ownership.

A FINAL THOUGHT

While this is a book about design, it's essential to remember materialism is not enough.

It cannot be overemphasised that success in the design of a building, especially one that exists to foster human connection, is contingent on the characters involved – not only in a scheme's genesis, but in the way a building is managed and the power of intention.

Endnotes

Introduction

1 Space10 and Urgent Agency, *Imagine, Exploring the Brave New World of Shared Living*, 2018.

2 United Nations, *World Urbanization Prospects: The 2018 Revision*, 2019.

3 Brie Weiler Reynolds, *159% Increase in Remote Work Since 2005: FlexJobs & Global Workplace Analytics Report*, Flexjobs, 2019.

4 Nicholas Bloom, James Liang, John Roberts and Zhichun Jenny Ying, 'Does Working from Home Work? Evidence from a Chinese Experiment,' *The Quarterly Journal of Economics*, February 2015, Vol.130, No.1, pp165–218.

5 Daniel Bentley and Alex McCallum, *Rise and Fall: The Shift in Household Growth Rates Since the 1990s*, Civitas, February 2019.

6 Sevil Peach, 'A conversation on the future of the workspace', *Vitra: A Safe Landing in a New Office Reality, The e-Paper About the Future of Work*, No.2, 2019.

Chapter 1

1 Space10 and Anton & Irene, *One Shared House 2030*, http://onesharedhouse2030.com (accessed 20 July 2020).

2 Raheel Mushtaq, et al, 'Relationship Between Loneliness, Psychiatric Disorders and Physical Health? A Review on the Psychological Aspects of Loneliness', *Journal of Clinical and Diagnostic Research*, Vol.8, No.9, September 2014.

3 UN Environment and International Energy Agency, 'Towards a zero-emission, efficient, and resilient buildings and construction sector', *UN Environment Global Status Report 2017*, 11 December 2017.

4 Office for National Statistics, *The Cost of Living Alone*, 4 April 2019.

5 'The Power of Privacy', *IKEA Life at Home Report 2019*, IKEA, 2019.

6 George Monbiot, 'The horror films got it wrong. This virus has turned us into caring neighbours', *Guardian*, 31 March 2020.

7 'Is coliving here to stay?', *Coliving Insights*, 30 June 2020, Vol.2, pp8–35.

8 'The Conscious Coliving Manifesto', *Conscious Coliving*, 29 January 2020.

9 Karl Tomusk, 'As WeWorks lie empty, coworking spaces face their day of reckoning', *Wired*, 28 May 2020.

Chapter 2

1 German Federal Statistical Office.

2 Rebecca Thandi Norman, 'How BaseCamp is solving the student housing crisis in style across Europe', *Wallpaper**, 24 August 2018.

3 Roos van Strien, 'How The Student Hotel Makes Millennials Pay for Amsterdam's Housing Shortage', *Failed Architecture*, 28 September 2017.

4 Insight Network, University Mental Health Survey 2018

5 Michael D Burnard and Andreja Kutnar, 'Wood and human stress in the built indoor environment: a review', *Wood Science and Technology*, 2015, No.49, pp969–986.

Chapter 3

1 Marcus Fairs, 'Student-style accommodation for adults is going to be the next market says Naomi Cleaver', *Dezeen*, 11 September 2015.

2 Jessica Mairs, 'World's largest co-living complex promises residents everything at their fingertips', *Dezeen*, 28 April 2016.

3 *Living Closer, The Many Faces of Co-Housing*, Studio Weave, June 2018, pp103–111.

4 Angelica Krystle Donati, 'Is Co-Living 2.0 The Next Big Thing In Residential Real Estate?', *Forbes*, 22 March 2019.

5 'Co-Living Startup "The Collective" is Forging a Bright Future During COVID-19', *Forbes*, 23 May 2020.

Chapter 4

1 Daniel Bentley and Alex McCallum, *Rise and Fall: The Shift in Household Growth Rates Since the 1990s*, Civitas, February 2019.

2 Eurofound, *Household Composition and Well-Being*, Publications Office of the European Union, Luxembourg, 2019.

3 United Nations, Department of Economic and Social Affairs, *Population Division, World Population Ageing 2017 Highlights*, 2017.

4 Office for National Statistics, *UK Private Rented Sector: 2018*, 18 January 2019.

5 Glen Bramley, *Housing Supply Requirements Across Great Britain for Low-Income Households and Homeless People: Research for Crisis and the National Housing Federation; Main Technical Report*, Heriot Watt University, April 2019.

6 Marie Stender, 'Social Living, Version 2.0, an ethnography of three new Danish residential complexes', *Nordic Journal of Architecture*, 2015.

7   Pollard Thomas Edwards and Levitt Bernstein Associates, *Housing our Ageing Population: Panel for Innovation (HAPPI)*, Homes and Communities Agency, 2009.

8   Office for National Statistics, *Living Longer: How Our Population is Changing and Why it Matters*, 2019.

9   Raheel Mushtaq, et al., 'Relationship Between Loneliness, Psychiatric Disorders and Physical Health? A Review on the Psychological Aspects of Loneliness', *Journal of Clinical and Diagnostic Research*, 2014, Vol.8, No.9.

10 Janice Turner, 'Is this the world's coolest old people's home?', *The Times Magazine*, 27 August 2016.

11 Humanitas Deventer, *Humanising Care, The Humanitas Deventer Workbook*, 2019.

Chapter 5

1   Office for National Statistics, 'Trends in self-employment in the UK', https://www.ons.gov.uk/employmentandlabourmarket/peopleinwork/employmentandemployeetypes/articles/trendsinselfemploymentintheuk/2018-02-07 (accessed 26 November 2020); Elaine Pofeldt, 'Survey: Nearly 30% of Americans Are Self-Employed', *Forbes*, 30 May 2020.

2   Coworking Resources, *Global Coworking Growth Study 2020*, 7 March 2020.

3   Emanuele Midolo, 'Don't blame coronavirus for WeWork's collapse, blame WeWork', *Wired*, 6 April 2020.

4   George Hammond, 'IWG looks to raise £315m war chest', *Financial Times*, 27 May 2020.

5   Oliver Pickup, 'The office isn't dead, it's different', *Raconteur*, 28 July 2020.

6   Mark Westall, 'Rohan Silva co-founder of Second Home', *FAD-Magazine*, 22 May 2018.

7   Number of people working in coworking spaces worldwide 2010–2020, statista.com.

8   Number of people working in coworking spaces worldwide in 2016 and 2017, by age group, statista.com.

9   Deskmag, 'Member Demographics – Members of Coworking Spaces – Part 1 – The 2017 Global Coworking Survey', https://www.slideshare.net/carstenfoertsch/members-of-coworking-spaces-demographic-background-global-coworking-survey-80058366 (accessed 19 November 2020).

10 Katherine Rosman, 'Audrey Gelman, the Wing's Co-Founder, Resigns', *The New York Times*, 11 June 2020.

11 Meredith Lepore, 'Audrey Gelman Is Reviving the Old-Fashioned Concept of Women's Clubs', *New York Observer*, 13 October 2016.

Chapter 6

1   Office for National Statistics, *Coronavirus and Homeworking in the UK: April 2020*, 2020.

2   Fiona Briggs, 'Bed overtakes sofa as the most used piece of furniture in British homes, Made.com reports', *Retail Times*, 22 September 2016.

3   United Nations, *World Urbanization Prospects: The 2018 Revision*, 2019.

Chapter 7

1   Robin Dunbar, *Human Evolution*, Pelican, 2014.

Index

Picture credits

Figs 0.0.1 and 3.0.2 Cohost West Bund

Figs 1.0.1, 3.2.1, 3.2.2, 3.2.3 and 3.2.4 Nicholas Worley

Figs 2.0.0, 2.4.8 a–c and 2.5.7 a–c Naomi Cleaver

Fig. 2.0.2 Scape

Fig. 2.0.3 BIG / Laurent de Carniere

Fig. 2.0.4 Kasia Gatkowska

Figs 2.1.1, 2.1.2, 2.1.3 and 2.1.4 Andy Matthews

Fig. 2.1.5 Tigg + Coll Architects

Figs 2.2.1, 2.2.2, 2.2.3, 2.2.4 and 2.2.5 Studio Aisslinger / Jens Bösenberg

Figs 2.3.1, 2.3.2, 2.3.3, 2.3.4 and 2.3.5 The Student Hotel / Sal Marston Photography

Figs 2.3.6 a–c The Student Hotel / Rizoma Architetture

Figs 2.4.1, 2.4.2, 2.4.3, 2.4.4, 2.4.5, 2.4.6, 2.4.7, 2.5.1, 2.5.2, 2.5.3, 2.5.4, 2.5.5, 2.5.6, 4.3.1, 4.3.2, 4.3.4, 4.3.5, 4.3.6, 4.3.7, 4.3.8, 4.3.9 and 7.0.5 Naomi Cleaver / Ed Reeve

Figs 3.0.0 and 3.0.4 Cohabs

Figs 3.0.1, 3.1.1, 3.1.2, 3.1.3, 3.1.4, 3.1.5 and 3.1.6 The Collective / Ed Reeve

Fig. 3.0.3, 3.5.1, 3.5.2, 3.5.3 and 3.5.4 LifeX

Figs 3.3.1, 3.3.2, 3.3.3, 3.3.4 and 3.3.5 Vivahouse

Figs 3.4.1, 3.4.2 and 3.4.3 K9 Coliving

Figs 3.6.1, 3.6.2, 3.6.3, 3.6.4 and 7.0.4 Cutwork Studio / Handover Agency

Fig. 3.6.5 Cutwork Studio

Figs 4.0.0, 4.4.1, 4.4.2, 4.4.3 and 4.4.5 Dorte Mandrup Arkitekter / Stamers Kontor

Fig. 4.0.1 David Butler

Fig. 4.0.2 Katherine Lu

Figs 4.0.3 and 4.0.4 EFFEKT Architects and Space10

Figs 4.1.1, 4.1.2, 4.1.3, 4.1.4 and 4.1.5 Ossip van Duivenbode

Figs 4.1.6 a–e BETA

Figs 4.2.1, 4.2.2, 4.2.3, 4.2.4, 4.2.5 and 4.2.6 Heiko Prigge

Figs 4.2.7 a–c Macdonald Wright Architects

Figs 4.4.6 and 4.4.7 Dorte Mandrup

Fig. 4.5.1 Galit Seligmann

Figs 4.5.2 and 4.5.3 Greater London Authority

Figs 4.5.4 and 4.5.5 Tim Crocker

Figs 4.5.6 a–c Pollard Thomas Edwards

Figs 4.6.1, 4.6.2, 4.6.3 and 4.6.4 Sander van Wettum

Figs 4.7.1, 4.7.2, 4.7.3, 4.7.4 and 4.7.5 Courtesy of Serenbe

Figs 5.0.0 and 5.0.2 The Office Group / Michael Sinclair

Fig. 5.0.1 Kevin Bruce Photos / Shutterstock.com

Fig. 5.0.3 Second Home / Iwan Baan

Fig. 5.0.4 Fosbury & Sons / Jeroen Verrecht

Figs 5.1.1, 5.1.2, 5.1.3, 5.1.4 and 5.1.5 Emily Andrews

Figs 5.2.1, 5.2.2, 5.2.3, 5.2.4, 5.2.5 and 7.0.0 Fosbury & Sons / Frederik Vercruysse

Figs 5.3.1, 5.3.2, 5.3.3, 5.3.4 and 7.0.2 Jim Newberry

Fig. 5.3.5 Aaron Lyles / PIXELLAB

Fig. 5.3.6 Zooco Estudio

Figs 5.4.1, 5.4.2, 5.4.3, 5.4.4 and 5.4.5 The Wing

Figs 5.5.1, 5.5.2, 5.5.3, 5.5.4 and 5.5.5 James Jones

Figs 5.5.6 a–d Squire & Partners

Figs 6.0.0, 6.2.1, 6.2.2, 6.2.3, 6.2.4, 6.2.5 and 6.2.6 Ewout Huibers for Concrete and Zoku

Fig. 6.0.1 TMB-Fotoarchiv / Steffen Lehmann

Figs 6.0.2 and 6.0.3 Nicholas Worley

Figs 6.1.1, 6.1.2, 6.1.3, 6.1.4 and 6.1.5 Teatum+Teatum / Luke Hayes

Figs 6.1.6 a–c Teatum+Teatum

Figs 6.3.1, 6.3.2, 6.3.3, 6.3.4 and 6.3.5 Relja Ivanic

Fig. 6.3.6 Vladimir Sretenovic

Figs 6.3.7 and 6.3.8 Autori

Figs 6.4.1, 6.4.2, 6.4.3, 6.4.4 and 6.4.5 Outpost

Fig. 7.0.1 Jens Bösenberg

Fig. 7.0.3 James Jones